Cas

Endorsements

"Informative, inspiring, and passionate—*Casting Nets* offers spiritual advice through fascinating personal anecdotes, Church teaching, and encouragement to be a people of prayer, pursuing holiness and reaching out in evangelization."

Donna-Marie Cooper O'Boyle, Eternal Word Television Network host, speaker, and award-winning author of twenty books

"Tony and Chris are a great team not only because of their knowledge of the Catholic faith, but especially because of their love for the Church and their zeal for souls. Their book is a powerful answer to the Holy Father's call for a New Evangelization."

Jason Evert, Catholic author and speaker, www.chastityproject.com

"Catholics everywhere are looking for practical tips to proclaim the Gospel, and to invite friends and family to know, love, and serve Jesus Christ and His Church. *Casting Nets* offers an easy-to-understand guide to the universal call for a New Evangelization."

Bishop James D. Conley, Diocese of Lincoln, Nebraska

"In his Letter to the Romans, St. Paul asks, 'How are they to believe in Him of whom they have never heard? And how are they to hear without a preacher?' What a pity it would be for someone to lose out on meeting Jesus Christ because we feel unqualified to share the Good News. In this powerful book, Chris Stewart and Tony Brandt provide the tools necessary to share Jesus with those around us. After reading it, you will not only feel a greater desire to evangelize, but you'll feel confident that you can do it. Highly recommended!"

Gary Zimak, Catholic speaker and author of Faith, Hope, & Clarity: How to Know God's Will

"If you have a desire to share your Catholic faith with neighbors and with family, with friends and with co-workers, with people who have left the Church and those who have never heard the Gospel, then *Casting Nets: Grow Your Faith by Sharing Your Faith* is a must read. Tony and Chris have years of experience in spreading the Good News, and through their humor, stories, and passion they share with us how to effectively bring others to Jesus Christ and His Catholic Church."

Chris Stefanick, Catholic author and speaker,
www.reallifecatholic.com

"Here is a practical guide to build confidence in sharing the Good News of our Catholic faith. *Casting Nets* helps us act on Jesus' instruction when he exhorts, 'What you received as a gift, you must give as a gift!' (Mt 10:8)."

Archbishop Paul S. Coakley,
Archdiocese of Oklahoma City

"It was Pope St. John Paul the Great, herald of the New Evangelization, who famously wrote, 'Faith is strengthened when it is given to others!'" In their new book, *Casting Nets: Grow Your Faith by Sharing Your Faith,* Catholic evangelists Chris Stewart and Tony Brandt masterfully capture and synthesize the meaning and power of these words, and present a compelling theology of evangelization that will encourage and inspire their readers to grow more deeply in their faith while at the same time equipping them to share it more effectively with others. Written in an eminently simple yet thoroughly engaging way, Chris and Tony skillfully present the key principles and practices that are essential for all evangelizers, which is precisely what every baptized Catholic is called to be. This is the kind of book that all pastors should put in the hands of their parishioners. You'd start a spiritual revolution in no time. It's called the New Evangelization.

Hector Molina, "The Motivangelist,"
international Catholic speaker and evangelist,
www.hectormolina.com

Grow Your Faith by Sharing Your Faith

Introducing The Seven Pillars of Effective Evangelization

Chris Stewart, M.T.S., and Tony Brandt

Our Sunday Visitor Publishing Division
Our Sunday Visitor, Inc.
Huntington, Indiana 46750

Nihil Obstat
Msgr. Michael Heintz, Ph.D.
Censor Librorum

Imprimatur
✠ Kevin C. Rhoades
Bishop of Fort Wayne-South Bend
January 26, 2015

The *Nihil Obstat* and *Imprimatur* are official declarations that a book is free from doctrinal or moral error. It is not implied that those who have granted the *Nihil Obstat* and *Imprimatur* agree with the contents, opinions, or statements expressed.

20 19 18 17 16 15 1 2 3 4 5 6 7 8 9

Our Sunday Visitor Publishing Division
Our Sunday Visitor, Inc.
200 Noll Plaza
Huntington, IN 46750

1-800-348-2440
bookpermissions@osv.com

ISBN: 978-1-61278-893-7 (Inventory No. T1680)
eISBN: 978-1-61278-895-1
LCCN: 2015940446

Cover design: Tyler Ottinger
Cover art: Shutterstock

Printed in the United States of America

CONTENTS

Introduction

We have been blessed to travel the country speaking about the joy of spreading the Gospel and training individuals, parishes, and dioceses how to effectively evangelize. We have had the opportunity to meet many Catholics who are truly living the Gospel dynamically. Those who are actively sharing their faith with family, friends, neighbors, and strangers seem to have the most joy. We see in them the experience that we have felt in our lives as well: living the Faith brings joy to our lives, sharing the Faith brings joy to other people's lives, and that in return increases our own joy.

We designed *Casting Nets* to help you reach out in joy and love to those you want to draw to Christ and the Church. We base our vision for evangelization on the story of Jesus and the great catch of fish in Luke 5. He instructed His fishermen friends, who had fished all night with no success, to "put out into the deep" and cast their nets for a catch. And they caught so many fish their nets were breaking. Jesus used this experience to announce that from then on His disciples would be fishers of men (and women). That's what we want to help you achieve. We want to inspire you to put out into the deep in all your relationships and "catch" people for the Lord with your joy and love.

In *Casting Nets* we present seven essential—tested and easy-to-implement—ways of bringing others to Christ. For more than a decade we have taught thousands of people these "Seven Pillars of Effective Evangelization." We have shown them that successfully sharing the Faith depends on our understanding and application of these principles, or

"Pillars": Prayerful, Invitational, Hospitable, Inspirational, Sacramental, Formational, and Missionful. *Casting Nets* explains the principle and the practice of each of these Pillars.

If you have picked up this book then you must have some sort of desire to evangelize others. Maybe you have already decided to share the Good News with a particular person, family member, friend, or co-worker. Maybe you just want to be able to spread the Faith to anyone who God might bring to your attention.

The Seven Pillars of Effective Evangelization will help you with either of these desires. But first we need to reflect on this desire to share your faith, a desire that was placed there by the Holy Spirit. This desire is something very good, something that must be grown. And it is something as true disciples of Jesus Christ we have a moral obligation to respond to.

Scripture and the Moral Obligation to Evangelize

Jesus Christ, the Second Person of the Trinity, became man with one very specific goal in mind: the salvation of humanity. However, after Jesus suffered, died, rose from the dead, and before ascending to the Father, He gave His Spirit to the apostles. And He commanded them to continue His mission, saying, "As the Father has sent me, even so I send you" (Jn 20:21), and "Go therefore and make disciples of all nations, baptizing them in the name of the Father, and of the Son, and of the Holy Spirit" (Mt 28:19).

Thus the task of bringing salvation to the world was given by Christ to the apostles and through them to all members of the Church. The laity, in particular, fulfill their Christian vocation by participating in this apostolic mission within the world. That mission includes not only living in holiness according to the teachings of Christ and the apostles (see Acts 2:42), but also bringing the Good News of Christ's salvation to others.

St. Paul stands as the first and finest example of this mission of evangelization. He understood the urgency of sharing the Good News with others. As he said: "For if I preach the gospel, that gives me no ground for boasting. For necessity is laid upon me. Woe to me if I do not preach the gospel!" (1 Cor 9:16). Likewise, all the faithful within the Church must do their part in this mission according to their unique role within the world. "Woe to [us] if [we] do not preach the gospel!"

In the Gospels we read a story of Jesus coming upon a fig tree while walking toward the city of Jerusalem (see Mt 21:18-22; Mk 11:12-14,20-25). Apparently Jesus was extremely hungry, because when He found no figs on the tree He cursed it, saying, "May no fruit ever come from you again!" (Mt 21:19). This curse proved to be the death of the fig tree.

Why was Jesus so severe with the fig tree? What was so terrible about it? After all, wasn't it a living tree? Perhaps it provided shade from the hot, summer sun for passersby or a home for birds to nest. However, this fig tree lacked one very important thing: figs. This tree failed to produce fruit.

The fruit of Christ's salvation grows when we live a life of prayer, follow the teachings of the Church, and live a sacramental life. This life is a gift of God and is itself a proclamation of the Gospel to others in our social environments. However, we must always strive for more. Can we ever say that we love God *enough*, that we give *enough* glory to God, or that we are holy *enough*? We must challenge ourselves to *more*. We must do our best to produce *more* fruit. If this new life in Christ is truly "the pearl of great price" (Mt 13:46, NABRE), we can expect to want to share it with others both in word and deed. Our proclamation sheds light on the cause and significance of this new life in Christ.

The Gospel of Mark provides us with another interesting detail to this story: "it was not the season for figs" (Mk 11:13). So what does that tell us? Jesus expects us to bear witness to our faith, to produce fruit *in season and out of season*. We must share our faith when it is easy and when it is difficult, to the stranger and to the friend, at work and in the home, times when we feel close to Our Lord and times when we feel distant from Him. There is no vacation from the obligation to evangelize, for we never know when the Savior of the World will be walking by to check our branches for fruit.

The Bishops and the Moral Obligation to Evangelize

The Church has always understood this mandate to sanctify humanity as the reason for her existence. However, in recent decades the pope and bishops have called for a new awareness of the need to evangelize and the universal call to every member of the Church. As Pope Paul VI wrote: "The presentation of the Gospel message is not an optional contribution for the Church. It is the duty incumbent on her by the command of the Lord Jesus, so that people can believe and be saved. This message is indeed necessary. It is unique. It cannot be replaced. It does not permit either indifference, syncretism or accommodation. It is a question of people's salvation."[1] Indeed, salvation is on the line, especially if we are not willing to offer Christ's saving grace to others.

Our very identity as followers of Christ is connected with our willingness to bring others to Him. St. John Paul II once said, "No Christian community is faithful to its duty unless it is missionary: either it is a *missionary community* or it is not even a *Christian community*."[2] If a person does not participate in the evangelization mandate then he or she will be, as declared by the Second Vatican Council, "useful neither to the Church nor to himself."[3]

If we are ever looking for a measuring stick for our own personal faith, then Pope Benedict XVI offered our desire to evangelize as the marker: "Indeed, every Christian community is born missionary, and it is precisely on the basis of the courage to evangelize that the love of believers for their Lord is measured."[4] Thus, when we look at the saints, we see them constantly working to bring everyone to Christ. Our love for God can be directly measured by our willingness to evangelize.

The *Catechism of the Catholic Church* also connects evangelization to our own salvation: "The disciple of Christ must not only keep the faith and live on it, but also profess it, confidently bear witness to it, and spread it: 'All however must be prepared to confess Christ before men and to follow him along the way of the Cross, amidst the persecutions which the Church never lacks.' Service of and witness to the faith is necessary for salvation."[5]

A challenge that Pope Benedict XVI set before us is the question of whether or not each one of us has done the most for our own salvation: "As Christians we should never limit ourselves to asking: how can I save myself? We should also ask: what can I do in order that others may be saved and that for them, too, the star of hope may rise? Then I will have done my utmost for my own personal salvation as well."[6]

Are we ready to do everything we can for our own salvation? Are we ready to do everything we can for another's salvation?

The Seven Pillars of Effective Evangelization

We have seen that evangelization is at the heart of the Church's identity; it is the reason she exists, and it is a task given to all its members. Therefore, evangelization cannot be put into a formula such as "do A, then B, and finally C, and then we will have effective evangelization." The bishops of the United States wrote: "The New Evangelization offers hope. Our hope is not in a program or philosophy but in the person of Jesus Christ, who comforts those who are burdened."[7] Thus we are offering "pillars" and not "steps." "Pillars" create the foundation that make "steps" possible.

The Seven Pillars are meant to be foundational attitudes or principles that will allow effective evangelization to take place. They show us what evangelization requires in order to work properly—namely:

- a certain level of awareness that the time to spread the Gospel is now and the place is everywhere;
- a heart that listens to the movements of the Holy Spirit and is ready to act upon those promptings;
- a mind that is formed by the teachings of the Church and is prepared to share those teachings with the world;
- and a will that is obedient to the Church and humble enough to bear sufferings in order to witness to the love that Christ has for humanity.

An individual, a family, a parish, a ministry, or an entire diocese—anyone can use *The Seven Pillars*. We can incorporate them into our current programs or our new programs. The pillars can shape the practice of a family or a parish council. Most importantly, they are foundational principles that must shape each of our lives.

We believe these principles are universal. We have seen them at work in every program or individual that was able to successfully bring the Good News to others. And we can find all of these pillars in the life of Jesus. Indeed, we ought to learn from the Master how we can best love people into the kingdom of God.

Pillar 1

PRAYERFUL—The Principle

A great story is told that St. Pius X once asked a group of cardinals, "What does the Church need today?" One cardinal answered, "Schools." More Catholic schools seemed like a reasonable answer. The Holy Father responded, "No." Another cardinal volunteered, "More churches." The Holy Father again responded, "No." Yet another cardinal answered, "Better recruitment of priests." His Holiness finally answered, "No. What we need are holy laymen." What the Church needs now is for all its members to seek holiness relentlessly. In order to obtain this holiness we have got to be first and foremost a people of prayer.

Every time Jesus had a decision to make or a momentous act coming up, He went to pray. Whether it was the beginning of His public ministry (see Mt 4:1-11), choosing the Twelve Apostles (Lk 6:12-15), before big miracles (Lk 5:16; Mk 1:35-37; 6:46), the Transfiguration (Lk 9:28-29), or before His suffering and death (Mt 26:36-45), Jesus was always seeking to communicate with His Father. Jesus was such a model of prayer that His disciples asked Him to teach them how to pray (Lk 11:1). It is often forgotten that Jesus even prayed intercessory prayer when He prayed for Peter (Lk 22:32) and when He prayed for us (Jn 17:20-26). Since Jesus chose to make prayer a part of His effective ministry, every effective evangelist must be a person steeped and overflowing in prayer in order to bring Jesus Christ to others.

There is a well-known adage that says, "You can't give what you don't have." This can apply to many things in life including evangelization. The goal of evangelization is to share with others the truth that is Jesus Christ, but if we are unfamiliar with what that truth means for our own lives, then we will not have the truth to share with others. The pressing question remains: How can we bring Christ to others if we do not know Christ? Prayer is the "place" where we encounter God and speak to Him about our deepest concerns and our most heartfelt desires. Prayer is where God speaks His truth to us. Prayer is where we become fully alive in Christ; it is where we find peace, comfort, confidence, mercy, and most importantly an unquenchable love.

We have to keep in mind what Dr. Scott Hahn shares: "God is more concerned with sanctifying me than He is with sanctifying others through me."[8] Obviously this does not mean we should not be evangelizing, but instead it means that there is a priority to this process. We fly on planes quite often and probably could recite the safety instructions by the flight attendants. The attendants instruct the passengers that "in the case of emergency secure your own oxygen mask before assisting others." We have to be breathing before we can help others. Once we are "breathing" a life of prayer, once we have these encounters in our interior life, we can then say "we have it." We have the life, love, and light of Christ. Once we *have it*, we can then *give it*.

In order to be disciples who are effective in our evangelization efforts we must intensify our effort of bringing ourselves closer to Christ. Pope Francis described this challenge for all evangelists:

> Spirit-filled evangelizers means evangelizers fearlessly open to the working of the Holy Spirit. At Pentecost, the Spirit made the apostles go forth from themselves and turned them into heralds of God's wondrous deeds, capable of speaking to each person in his or her own language. The Holy Spirit also grants the courage to proclaim the newness of the Gospel with boldness (*parrhesía*) in every time and place, even when it meets with opposition. *Let us call upon him today, firmly rooted in prayer, for without prayer all our activity risks being fruitless and our message empty.* Jesus wants evangelizers who proclaim the good news not only with words, but above all by a life transfigured by God's presence.[9]

The principle is absolutely clear and concrete; prayer and evangelization are inseparable, sanctity and the New Evangelization are parallel.

I (Tony) had an experience in which I forgot the all-important connection about prayer and the work of the Holy Spirit in efforts of my evangelization. When I worked the *Totus Tuus Summer Camps*, all summer long I gave the confession preparation talks for the junior high or high school campers. After a summer of this I felt that I really had the talk down pat, which developed into an attitude that preparation was no longer even needed. Toward the end of the summer I again gave the talk without preparation or even without praying before the talk. Perhaps in my mind I had even justified that other tasks took priority over praying for the talk. I felt like I had nailed the talk, with passion, energy, and flow. I believed I hit every point needed to make the talk flawless. After the campers went to confession that night, however, the priest came out of the confessional and told me that I needed to redo the entire confession talk. The confessions he heard seemed to lack depth and heart.

I didn't understand. After all, I had the talk down perfectly, and it went well so many times before. So I started over and, as always, went back to prayer as with any new talk. But, I was coming up blank and becoming more and more stressed. The next week, when I had to give the confession talk, it was terrible! I came up with a stupid analogy about a fish that smokes cigars in his fish bowl and the water needed to be changed, but he wouldn't let anyone change it because it was comfortable to him. Just take my word for it, it was really bad. This time, however, the priest came out of the confessional crying and said the talk nailed it. The Holy Spirit was truly present and hearts had been changed that night. I was able to look back and realize it wasn't me, but the Holy Spirit who was now fully at work. I had been getting in the way of being the instrument of God's plan in the lives of the young people.

Dom Jean-Baptiste Chautard, a great spiritual writer of the twentieth century, explained the drastically different impact a holy priest and a decent priest will have on the people around them. While the following quote from his book is in reference to priests, we can replace the word "priest" with whomever we are or whatever we do, such as "teacher," "catechist," "youth minister," "parent," "grandparent," "godparent," "confirmation sponsor," "volunteer," "co-worker," or "neighbor." Chautard says:

> If the priest is a saint (the saying goes), the people will be fervent; if the priest is fervent, the people will be pious; if the priest is pious, the people will be at least decent. But if a priest is only decent, the people will be godless. The spiritual generation is always one

> degree less intense in its life than those who beget it in Christ.[10]

This places a large weight on our shoulders. Instead of just throwing our hands up in the air declaring that the "world is going to hell in a handbasket," maybe it is time to look inward to our own pursuit of holiness.

There is a real tendency for those in the Church to constantly be looking for the next program or method that is going to inspire those in the pews or call in the masses from the streets. However, no program is going to save this culture; neither will any governments, economic system, or medical research. The Savior of the World goes by one name, and that name is Jesus Christ. Evangelization is us, making Him present now, today. The only way that will happen is if we are a people of prayer, people striving for holiness.

While attempting to evangelize it is always easy to explain away lack of acceptance or enthusiasm for the Gospel message with the pretext that people have free will. While this excuse is easy to use, can we say that a misdirected free will is the *only* reason that people do not accept the Gospel? Did not the thousands of people converted by St. Francis Xavier, St. Francis de Sales, St. John Bosco, or Blessed Teresa of Calcutta also have free will? Of course they did. So what was the difference? We can come to only one conclusion: the instrument is different. Now, obviously, it is only grace that can move someone to accept the Good News of salvation, but we cannot help but think that those who are standing in front of us would be more open to grace if we were replaced by St. John Bosco or Blessed Teresa of Calcutta. Why is that? Because of the holiness of these saints, and because they knew and loved Christ more than we do. As Dom Chautard put it so sternly, "Educators [that is, anyone who brings the Gospel to others], because we lack an intensive inner life, are unable to beget in souls anything more than a surface piety, without any powerful ideals or strong convictions."[11]

Does this describe the success we have seen in our own work in the vineyard, in our apostolate? Of course, we still need to study; still need to come up with new, engaging stories; still need new ways to grab the attention of our audiences so that they might turn their ears to the message of God's grace. But what grace will reach them if we are a dry well versus a channel that the life of God rushes through?

The Sea of Galilee is the lowest freshwater lake in the world and is the second lowest lake. The Sea of Galilee is brimming with life both within its waters and on its shores. This is evident not only today but also from the Gospel stories that we are so familiar with about the fishing industry that was so abundant at the time of Christ (especially when the carpenter's son was giving the advice of where to fish in Luke 5:4).The Dead Sea, on the other hand, is appropriately named since its salt levels (about 35 percent) are so high that no life can exist except some bacteria and fungi. It is the lowest lake in the world and the shores are the lowest dry land in the world. My (Chris) wife was blessed to go to the Holy Land a few years ago and she visited the Dead Sea, and she recounted the strict instructions of the tour guide about not drinking even a little bit of the Dead Sea water. There was a prior instance, the guide advised, where a visitor ingested about a cup of this salt water and was rushed to intensive care where he stayed for a month because his kidneys were shutting down. Now, the distance between the two seas (actually lakes) is about sixty-five miles, and they are both fed by the same source, the Jordan River. So what is the cause of the difference between life and death in the two bodies of water? It seems to be that the Sea of Galilee has an outlet and the Dead Sea has none. In other words, the Jordan River flows into the Sea of Galilee and then it flows out, but not so with the Dead Sea, the water simply evaporates (about seven million tons a day), thus leaving the high concentration of salt. The lesson for us is that as Christ pours His grace within us so we must give that grace to others, we must produce fruit, or we will be at risk of being "cut down and thrown into the fire" (Mt 7:19).

The goal is to be a reservoir that takes in water in order to store it, that it may be distributed when needed. A reservoir ceases to be a good reservoir if, like the Dead Sea, it does not give out its life-giving water. But if all a reservoir does is give out its water and keeps nothing of itself, it is called a channel. To be a channel while evangelizing is a dangerous position, because the channel retains no grace for itself and eventually will dry up. What a delicate balance between keeping our reservoirs filled with the grace of God and continually giving ourselves to others.[12] It is a difficult balance, but it must be reached for the health of our soul and those who we are trying to reach. We can take the example of the saints and even Our Lord, who continually pulled away from the active work to draw close to the Source of all activity through solitude and prayer.

PRAYERFUL—The Practice

In order to effectively evangelize we must be a people of prayer. We must pursue holiness relentlessly so that our heart and mind are one with God. It is in prayer that our heart and mind are conformed to God's heart and mind. Pope Francis explains how prayer makes us better evangelists:

> One form of prayer moves us particularly to take up the task of evangelization and to seek the good of others: it is the prayer of intercession. Let us peer for a moment into the heart of St. Paul, to see what his prayer was like. It was full of people: "…I constantly pray with you in every one of my prayers for all of you … because I hold you in my heart" (Phil 1:4,7). Here we see that intercessory prayer does not divert us from true contemplation, since authentic contemplation always has a place for others.[13]

We must recommit ourselves to a renewal of an effective prayer life. To effectively evangelize we need a prayer life that has ***Passion, Purpose,*** and ***Perseverance***.

We must RE-commit to our prayer life with ***Passion***. Pray for an intense renewal in our own life and our own faith. The first step in the New Evangelization is a requirement on our part to continually be evangelized and renew our commitment to Christ. As Pope Francis exhorted:

> I invite all Christians, everywhere, at this very moment, to a renewed personal encounter with Jesus Christ, or at least an openness to letting him encounter them; I ask all of you to do this unfailingly each day. No one should think that this invitation is not

meant for him or her, since "no one is excluded from the joy brought by the Lord."[14]

If we have not made a firm commitment to daily personal prayer, then today must be that day. If we have a daily prayer life, then, can we take it to the next level? Can we get to daily Mass more often? Can we get to adoration more often? The New Evangelization will not be possible without this reNEWal in us.

During my (Chris') senior in high school my mother received the devastating news that she had breast cancer. I still vividly remember my mother on her bed crying while she still held the phone that had delivered the message. Unfortunately, this was at a time in my life in which I did not take my faith seriously; I was not a good Catholic, not a good son, not even a good citizen. But this news shook me to the core. I remember praying for the first time in years. Even though my prayers were shallow and selfish, I believe it began to open my heart a little. Praise God, my mother has been cancer free for twenty years. When we come face to face with the serious crisis of a family member or a close friend, such as a cancer diagnosis or news of a bad car accident, our prayers become intensely serious. We will pray with every fiber of our being and with all our strength begging God to intervene.

This is a good thing; indeed our heavenly Father desires to hear all the petitions that weigh so heavily on our hearts, but do we pray for conversions with the same intensity and passion? While physical healings may not always be in the will of God, we can be certain that God wants all people to enjoy eternal life with Him. After all, the conversion of sinners is what causes joy in heaven (see Lk 15:7,10). Praying for conversions in others is truly loving them, whether for family, friends, neighbors, strangers, or our enemies. Pope Francis encourages us to pray for everyone: "We all have our likes and dislikes, and perhaps at this very moment we are angry with someone. At least let us say to the Lord: 'Lord, I am angry with this person. I pray to you for him and for her.' To pray for a person with whom I am irritated is a beautiful step forward in love, and an act of evangelization. Let us do it today! Let us not allow ourselves to be robbed of the ideal of fraternal love!"[15] In the Bible, Jesus counsels us with this instruction: "Love your enemies and pray for those who persecute you" (Mt 5:44). The first step to the act of forgiveness is praying for them, which will lead us then to doing acts of charity for them.

Consider this example from my family's (Chris') experience. There was once a person in our neighborhood who didn't like the barking of any dogs. We have a rat terrier who loves to bark with her high-pitched, annoying bark. Every time Teri would begin to bark, the neighbor would put a foghorn out the window and blare it. It became quite a contentious situation. My wife decided that for the feast of St. Thérèse of Lisieux—the Little Flower—she and the kids were going to hand out flowers with "God loves you" written on them throughout several neighborhoods. The kids went hesitantly to the door of this person and gave her a flower of love, and a miracle happened that day! She has never blown that foghorn since and actually called recently to say that our gate door was open and she was afraid Teri might get out. That is the power of prayer and action!

Pray for a heart like our Savior, a heart full of zeal and love for lost souls. Pray with intensity that Our Lord will open our eyes, ears, and lips to love others into the Kingdom. When this becomes our prayer it will be amazing how often we will begin to see opportunities to share the Good News. When I (Chris) was visiting a friend in San Diego, he was generous enough to take me—a guy raised in Kansas—surfing. (I am sure it was just for his own entertainment). After I had adequately embarrassed myself and we were done with the suffering, we enjoyed watching the sun set over the ocean while sitting around a small campfire on the beach. A young couple came on the beach looking for their own fire pit, but there were none left, so we invited them to join us. As the couple was gathering their wood, my friend, who has a passion for saving souls, led us in a quick prayer: "Father, if we can be an instrument for this couple to come to know You then let us be that instrument. Hail Mary, full of grace…" No exaggeration, within the first five minutes of the conversation we were talking about Christ and His Church with the couple. She was a non-practicing Catholic, and he was someone raised with no religion. I will never forget that prayer or conversation, or the example that my friend showed me for having a passion for saving souls (that friend went on to become a chastity speaker, reaching millions of souls across the world). Pray for passion to pray with passion to be the evangelist that brings souls to Christ to satisfy His passion.

We must RE-commit to our prayer life with ***Purpose***. A prayer life that has purpose will demonstrate commitment. Faithfulness to a daily prayer time is essential. Do we give at least one percent of our day to the Lord? In a twenty-four-hour day, one percent is only fifteen minutes. Do we give the Lord the best time slots of our day or the leftovers? At our (Chris') home we have what we call a "prayer chair." It is well-worn, complete with foam falling out of its arms, but it is the first place that we begin every morning. My wife and I read the Scriptures in that chair every morning. Daily Scripture reading is so essential to our prayer life to allow Our Lord to speak to us through His Word. This kind of committed prayer life will make clear our purpose as evangelists.

We need to pray for, by name, those who we want to come into or come back into the Church. Do not be afraid to be specific. When I (Chris) was driving to visit a Methodist minister, who had become a good friend because of his influence on me during my years in college where he was the chaplain, I was praying a Rosary for him and our conversation. In my prayer I asked the Blessed Mother to allow me to ask him one question, then she could have the rest of the conversation. (I was so generous.) The one question I wanted to ask the minister was, "How is your prayer life going?" When I arrived at the small college we quickly caught up. "How are things going?" "How's the family?" "How's work going?" Then the Methodist minister asked me, "So, Chris, how is your prayer life going?" I picked myself up from the floor and proceeded to describe to him what was going on in my prayer life and where I would like to be. Then without me saying a word, he went on to describe his own prayer life and that was the entirety of the conversation. Purposeful prayer can change lives.

Be open to the Holy Spirit and ask the Spirit to suggest people to pray for, then pray for them regularly and watch for opportunities to encourage them with your words. We know people who carry a piece of paper with a list of names of those that they are praying for. Use your phone calendars to remind you when to send a text or call someone needing prayers that day. People, above all, want to be noticed and wanted. So, being mindful of what is important to others is key to purpose-filled prayer in action.

When our prayer has purpose it will make its way to every part of our day. If we are about to have a conversation in which sharing the Gospel could happen, then we need to pray before it. This could be a silent prayer on our own, or we could invite the other person to pray with us. When conversations about the Faith happen spontaneously then perhaps we can end with prayer, as Pope Francis encourages us:

> If it seems prudent and if the circumstances are right, this fraternal and missionary encounter could end with a brief prayer related to the concerns which the person may have expressed. In this way they will have an experience of being listened to and understood; they will know that their particular situation has been placed before God, and that God's word really speaks to their lives.[16]

Prayer can be simple encouragements to those around us. When an evangelist prays with purpose it can give purpose to our day, and then the lives around us might find their true purpose.

We must RE-commit to our prayer life with ***Perseverance***. Never lose heart; always trust that the King of All Hearts will hear this prayer. As Pope Benedict XVI said, "It is never too late to touch the heart of another, nor is it ever in vain."[17] Can we imagine what might have happened if St. Monica had stopped after five years of praying for her son, Augustine? So many times after our talks parents and grandparents approach us with stories about family members who are no longer practicing their faith. Their broken hearts break ours because everyone has family member and friends in this state. We also encourage them to never stop praying, and we share with them the prayers we wrote. The first is to St. Monica:

> St. Monica, as you prayed so faithfully for your son's conversion to Christ for many years, I ask for your intercession as I pray for (Name). Please grant them, by the power of the Holy Spirit clarity of mind and purity of heart according to the Truth of Jesus Christ, so that they will have the courage and conviction to live in knowledge, love, and service of Jesus Christ in this life and the next.

While Monica prayed unceasingly for Augustine, it was Ambrose, not she, who would be the effective instrument to bring Augustine to Christ. So we also share this Prayer to St. Ambrose:

> St. Ambrose, you were sent as an answer to the prayers of St. Monica for the conversion of her son, St. Augustine. I now humbly plead for your intercession, to send someone, like you were to St. Augustine, into the life of (Name). May they be led to know our Lord and Savior, Jesus Christ, and the truth of His Most Holy Church. I pray that I may be a fit instrument in and not an obstacle to their conversion, and that I may have the wisdom to see the difference.[18]

St. Monica was rewarded for her persistent prayer with the conversion of her son St. Augustine, and the Church was given one of the greatest minds of two thousand years. Prayer that is persistent can change the world.

Since we believe in the power of persistent prayer, we developed the "Casting Nets Prayer Crew," who are people that pray Memorares for our ministry and those that Casting Nets will encounter. We developed "business cards" and "postcards" with the Memorare and a number grid that allows the person to count up to one thousand Memorares. Then they give us the card and we take those prayers wherever we go. We encourage the "Crew Member" to add their own intentions and share those prayers with others. Here is one such story from a friend of ours:

> My sister recently went through a very difficult divorce. She married an atheist who, along with her own personal struggles, led her away from her Catholic faith. Her incredibly miserable marriage led her to incredible loneliness. This misery led her back to prayer, and she is going to a Christian church with her two boys now. Life has been and continues to be very difficult for her. I prayed one thousand Memorares over a ten-day period for her and for her sons and sent the Casting Nets Prayer Crew Card to her with a personal letter. I never expect a response when I do this because many times I do not get a response. My sister, whom I rarely talk to, called me to personally thank me for the letter and the prayers. She called me in tears and said she hasn't received a hand written letter in the mail since she was a child. She was incredibly grateful. Shocked at the words personally written for her, she was overjoyed! So often we don't get an update on the effects of our prayers in real time, and this was one of those special moments.

When the evangelist prays with perseverance the heart of our loving Father will be captured and the perseverance will prove our love for friends, family, and strangers so that they may be granted the perseverance to gain a true conversion, for "Love never fails" (1 Cor 13:8, NABRE)!

There will never be a New Evangelization without a new commitment to a life of prayer and relentless pursuit of holiness. As we renew our relationship with Jesus Christ, His wants will become our wants. His zeal for souls will become our zeal for souls. His desire to invite all people into communion with Him will become our desire to invite all to Him. Remarkably, our focus to turn inward to find the King of the Universe will ultimately turn us outward to the world around us to share the Person and relationship we have found and invite all to the same Good News.

Pillar 2

INVITATIONAL—The Principle

Jesus compared the kingdom of heaven to a wedding feast (see Mt 22:1-14). The king prepared a huge feast, which must have taken much time and many resources. He sent servants to bring the guests he had personally invited, but they refused to come, which did not go well for them. The king did not rest his passion to have the wedding hall full. He sent his servants back out to the highways and byways to invite personally the good and the bad to come enjoy the feast. This parable is still playing out today; we are the servants carrying this invitation to the Table of the Lord to every street we visit. Like the king in the parable, Jesus himself invited people personally.

When most of us imagine Jesus' public ministry, we usually see Him surrounded by throngs of people. Indeed Jesus spoke to large crowds and came to redeem *all* of humanity: "Come to me, all who labor and are heavy laden, and I will give you rest" (Mt 11:28) and "Let the children come to me, and do not hinder them; for to such belongs the kingdom of God" (Lk 18:16). Jesus invited all, but He is also a *personal* Savior. Jesus personally invited the apostles by name (see Mt 9:9, Lk 5:1-11, Jn 1:43-51). He had individual conversations with Nicodemus (Jn 3:1-21), the young rich man (see Mk 10:17-22), the Samaritan woman at the well (Jn 4:4-41), and the woman caught in adultery (Jn 8:1-11). After the Resurrection,

Jesus invited the apostles to an intimate breakfast with Him (Jn 21:12). When Jesus miraculously healed someone, it was almost always individually. Jesus was continually inviting, and He was inviting individually.

It is so easy to get caught up in the numbers game; obviously, we think the more people who show up the better we must be doing. We want to convert all of our family and friends. We want our pews to be full and all our events to be packed. Jesus was not worried about numbers. Jesus worked many miracles, but how many blind people died while never seeing the light of day while Jesus walked the earth? How many lepers died around the world during Jesus' three years of public ministry? If Jesus was concerned about numbers, He went about it in a funny way. Blessed Teresa of Calcutta said: "Never worry about numbers. Help one person at a time and start with the person nearest you." We want everyone to be Catholic, but let's begin with inviting one person at a time. Imagine if everyone in your parish invited just one person a month to an event at the church? Sure there would be many rejections, but we imagine that it might not be long before a building project would be necessary.

For the most part, the efforts of parishes across the country to invite people to the church are small at best:

- Bulletin announcements are not going to get the job done. Let's be very clear, bulletins and announcements before or after Mass *are not* invitations. They simply announce an event or better yet serve as a reminder to those who were already planning on attending.

- A great looking, modern website *is not* an invitation; most visitors to parish websites are already members of the parish.
- Signage outside of our churches on the street *are not* invitations. They might give the impression that we don't mind new people showing up, but is someone who has never stepped foot in our church going to come to the parish mission because we put the time and title of a talk on a sign?
- Statues of the Blessed Virgin Mary or St. Francis of Assisi *are not* invitations to our neighbors that we want to talk about Catholicism with them. Those statues might just explain why we are not home Sunday morning.
- Catholic T-shirts *are not* invitations to the Gospel. They can be conversation starters.

All the items just mentioned are necessary activities, but do not be confused on who may benefit from them; it is mainly the current members of the parish. We have seen some parishes and dioceses use billboards, radio, and even television commercials to invite the lost to come home. This is important work and more resources need to be given so that Catholic apostolates can do this well. However, keep in mind that we want to be like our Savior and also use personal invitations.

A personal invitation has power. It carries weight, and it means something. A simple personal invitation implies many things behind the invitation to the person invited. When I invite someone it lets them know "I was thinking of *you*." It implies, "I want *you* there." A personal invitation reveals to the invitee, "I think *you* would enjoy it." The invitation shows, "I care enough about *you* to ask *you*." This is why all of us love to be invited. If we hear of an event that we were not invited to, we may feel left out, as if something was wrong with us.

In preparing for another week of Totus Tuus (a parish vacation Bible school) my (Chris') wife, Maria, told me she was going to invite the two neighbor kids to the week. At the time we did not know these neighbors very well and to our knowledge they were not regular churchgoers. A few minutes later Maria came back excited with the news that they were going to participate in the week. That following Easter the children entered the Church and we were honored to be the godparents of one of them, all because of the simple invitation to a youth summer program.

So if personal invitations can have such a huge impact on individuals then why don't we invite more often? For most it comes down to four reasons: fear, confidence, time, or judging.

The first reason is fear of rejection or from being told no. What do we really have to be afraid of? It could be that we are afraid of being told no, but this seems unlikely since we do not have any fear of this when inviting someone to a dinner, movie, birthday party, or wedding. Perhaps the fear is a concern of being thought of as intolerant or pushy. Remember that by inviting we are not imposing our faith but simply proposing. When we send out wedding invitations we are not forcing the guests to come, are we? Normally, we don't send out fewer wedding invitations because we worry about rejection.

Even if there is fear it needs to be overcome. Like most people I (Chris) have a fear of getting a traffic ticket.

During a family birthday party our daughter, Teresa, was outside playing tag in the fading sunlight. She came around the corner and tripped over a neighbor kid. It was obvious Teresa had broken her arm in the fall. We got in the car to drive to the emergency room. The first red light we hit I looked both ways and went through. The love of my first-born child pushed away the fear of getting a ticket. Let's not allow our emotions to get in the way of invitation. If we love those people, then fear will not stop us from inviting them to something so great.

The second reason we may not invite is because we lack confidence. When it comes to the work of evangelization we need to realize whose work it is. Evangelization is the work of the Holy Spirit. It is our job to invite and the Holy Spirit's job to move hearts. We are not asking you to share what you do not know but to share what you do know. When God commissions He also equips. Keep in mind this expression, "God does not call the qualified, He qualifies the called." If we wait until we are ready, then we will never be ready. The apostles would have been stuck in the Upper Room and the Israelites would still be in Egypt because Moses would never have been ready. Our confidence is not in the person bringing the Good News; our confidence is placed *in* the Good News.

The third reason we may not invite is because of lack of time. We are just too busy. In fact, one of the most common responses to "how are you?" has become "busy." First of all, this shows why the personal invitation is so powerful: you have been making time to think of them. But invitations are not that time-consuming in the grand scheme of life. We are encouraging you to simply invite people to those events you were thinking of attending anyway. If you are going to go on the parish retreat, who else can you take with you? If you are going to enjoy "coffee & donuts" after the Sunday Mass, is there a family in church that you can invite to come with you? Invitations take minutes but can change lifetimes.

The fourth reason we may not invite is because we have already prejudged or assumed what a person's answer is going to be. We think we "know" them; we think we "know" what they would say, or we think we "know" what they were doing last weekend. But we truly never know what God might be doing in someone's life. We can never really know what he or she is thinking or what is going on in his or her life. Maybe last night our neighbor was lying in bed thinking, "I want something new. God help me." Will you be the one to invite them?

The salvation of humanity has been placed in the hands of the Church, in our hands. In a very real sense we are "gatekeepers" of the Salvation of Jesus Christ. If we do not invite, the gates of heaven will be closed for many. Our job as gatekeepers is to keep the gates wide open and bring as many people as possible to the doorstep. Are we ready and willing to invite as many people as possible to the very gates of the kingdom of God?

INVITATIONAL—The Practice

There was a murder at the radio station where we have recorded our weekly show for the past two years. The young man who was killed was our show's producer. Daniel was a good kid who loved what he was doing in the radio business. He shared with us his hopes of one day being on the other side of the mic talking about the sports teams he loved, but, unfortunately, he never got that chance. When Tony and I heard the news it was heartbreaking. I asked Tony, "Do you think we did enough?" Daniel had been raised Catholic but had been struggling with getting to Sunday Mass with his duties at the radio station, which led to distancing himself from the Church. Tony knew what I was asking; he knew I was asking if we had done enough with encouraging Daniel to get back into his faith. Tony answered, "No … probably not." With tears in our eyes we drove home in silence.

When it comes to the immediacy of our invitations, there is no tomorrow. Jesus Christ wants every person possible to experience His grace, mercy, and forgiveness, and to enter the gates of the kingdom of God into eternal life. In order for that to happen, it is our job during the short life that we have to invite as many people as possible to the gates of heaven before it is too late.

For our invitations for evangelization to be effective they must be ***Personal***, ***Practical***, and ***Persistent***.

Invitations are ***Personal*** by their nature, but we need to be sure to make them personal.

When I (Tony) was walking down the hall of the high school where I teach, I saw a student sitting on the floor against the locker. Phil was a student who spent a lot of time kicked out of class. We all know a "Phil." He was the student who did not just fail to know where the line was, he would do a cartwheel into the classroom in order to cross over the line in style. I sat down next to Phil in the hallway and said, "How's it going?" He looked at me and answered, "Fine." I asked again but with more sincerity and meaning. "No really, how are you doing, for real?"

He then looked at me and told me that no one had ever really asked him that before. So I said: "It sounds like you have a lot to talk about, I would love to hear all about it. I will be at IHOP at six tomorrow morning, and I will buy you breakfast and hear what you have to say. I will be there no matter what. I hope to see you there." Now, granted, I love breakfast, but I was not expecting Phil to show up. He couldn't even show up to school on time. When I showed up at IHOP at 6:00 a.m. he was waiting for me.

We continued to develop a good relationship over the next couple of years, but there was too much working against him. Phil was eventually kicked out of school and slowly I lost track of him. Several years later, walking up to a local convenience store, I saw some kids loitering outside it. One looked up at me and flicked his cigarette down to greet me with a "Hello, Mr. Brandt." It was Phil. I asked him how he was doing and he responded that he wasn't doing that great, but he was trying to make some changes. I told him I would pray for him and that was that.

Years later after that encounter, a young lady got up to talk at the end of Mass about some retreats she had been on and to encourage the youths in the congregation to go on an upcoming one. After Mass she approached me to tell me that one of the counselors on the retreat wanted to say hello to me. I couldn't believe it when she told me it was Phil! It was truly a blessing to see the fruit of this personal invitation.

An invitation must be ***Practical***. A practical invitation is one that fits the person who we are inviting. In our secular life this is a no-brainer. We would not invite someone who has no interest at all in sports to a professional football game, or we would not invite someone who does not know us at all to help us move our furniture from one room to another. We need to think in the same terms when inviting in our faith life.

Someone who has not set foot in a church in ten years may not be ready to be on the parish council but may be open to a parish fish fry. Someone who has been brought up in a different faith tradition may not be open to a parish mission but may be open to a Bible study in a parishioner's home. Someone who attends Sunday Mass simply out of an obligatory habit may not be ready to lead the youth group but may be open to a parish retreat.

More than ten years ago Tony asked me, "Do you think we could get some high school guys to go to Mass one more time a week?" I answered, "Whew, that's asking a lot, but I know it would have to involve food." So we began to personally invite guys to come to a Thursday evening Mass and then to have dinner and hang out. If a guy continued to show up on Thursday, then we invited him to a weekend retreat we held once in the winter and once in the summer. As those relationships grew we then invited the young man to be "knighted," which included a total consecration to Jesus Christ through Mary. At each step we were discerning, asking for the help of the Holy Spirit to be able to offer invitations to the right opportunities at the right time. We have been blessed to witness more than two hundred young men join the Knights of the Holy Queen and strive for holiness in a group of brotherly accountability. It all started with a simple practical invitation.

And our invitations must be ***Persistent***. If we believe someone would really enjoy a restaurant, movie, or song, we do not hesitate in inviting them again and again until they at least try that restaurant, watch that movie, or listen to that song. We do not want to nag, but we want our friends to know we really do believe they will enjoy what we enjoy. Jesus gave us the example of the friend banging on the door at midnight which will wake up his friend inside simply out of persistence (see Lk 11:5-13). If we believe the Good News is the best thing that could happen to our family, friends, co-workers, or strangers, then we must persistently invite them.

There was a young man I (Tony) really wanted to be a part of the Knights of the Holy Queen. He was a stud athlete being recruited to play Division I college football, so I asked if he would come to Mass on Thursday and hang out with us. His first response was, "Oh, I'm sorry Mr. Brandt, I have some homework." So I asked the next week. "Sorry, Mr. Brandt, but I promised my girlfriend we would watch a movie." And the next. "Sorry, Mr. Brandt, I need to wash my car." After a few more weeks of this invitation the young man finally said, "Mr. Brandt, I'm sorry, I just don't want to go." That may or may not have been the first truthful excuse he gave me. So I stopped inviting him … for a little while. Toward the end of his senior year he showed up to Mass on Thursday evening, saying: "I'm ready. I'm all in and tired of being fake." And he was. That young man went on to play football at a public university where he began his own young men's group similar to the Knights of the Holy Queen. His roommate converted to Catholicism, and by his senior year in college it was his responsibility to lead the football team in prayer.

It all started with a persistent invitation to Mass on a Thursday night.

In all of this we are taking our cue from our loving God. Take, for example, the famous story of Peter's encounter with Jesus after the Resurrection in John 21. Jesus called Simon by name as He does each of us. Jesus accepts Peter where he is at currently, which is a fallen man who had denied even knowing Jesus, but Jesus is calling Peter to more. Indeed, Peter will eventually be able lay down his life for faith in Jesus. Our Lord takes each of us exactly where we are, but is always calling us to something more. Jesus then asks Peter to "follow Him" again, which was the original call Peter received at the beginning of Jesus' public ministry.

Our Lord will never give up on us; He is always knocking at the door (see Rev 3:20). So we must be like our loving God to use invitations that are personal, practical, and persistent so that everyone will know they are always welcomed at the banquet table (Lk 14:15-24).

Pillar 3

HOSPITABLE—The Principle

A friend of ours shared this story about how she came back home to the Catholic Church. Audrey was raised Catholic but, like so many of us today, at some point left her faith behind. It had been years since she had entered a church, and the first church she set foot in was Methodist. She quietly slipped into the back pew, trying not to be noticed. As the service began with the opening hymn, the gentleman next to her opened his hymnal and extended his arm out so that Audrey could sing along. This simple act made her feel at home and she began to attend that church. And, through the grace of God, she later returned to the Catholic faith. A simple act of hospitality became the catalyst that changed her life.

To say that Jesus displayed the virtue of hospitality would be somewhat of an understatement. He welcomed everyone. Jesus' displays of hospitality were such that they upset some people. We see Jesus eating with the tax collectors (see Mt 9:10) and the Pharisees (Lk 7:36). Jesus broke cultural norms by sharing a cup of water with a Samaritan woman (Jn 4:7-9) and by being willing to enter the house of a centurion (Lk 7:4-6). He took time to speak with the well-educated (Jn 3:1-21), and yet He had time for the children (Mt 19:14). When Zacchaeus was looking for Jesus, it turned out that Jesus was looking for him (Lk 19:1-10). In the presence of Jesus, everyone could feel welcomed.

Hospitality is one virtue that Catholics are notoriously lacking. I (Chris) must have been in fifth grade when one weekend my mother and I went to a Saturday vigil Mass at a parish on the other side of town. We walked into the foyer of the church, where two greeters met us and said, "Welcome to St. Francis, we are glad you're here tonight." My mother was so startled that she asked the greeters, "Are we at the Catholic church?" Funny, but both a true and a sad story.

If people do not feel welcomed when they arrive at our church, then our invitations will be meaningless. Outside a special gift of grace, the chance of someone coming back to our church is extremely small if he or she does not make or have a personal connection with someone there. And yet how do we make strangers feel at our churches when we see them? When someone steps foot into our churches, campuses, or homes, they need to know that this is where they belong. This is what they have been longing for, and that they have found it.

Southern hospitality is very well-known, but if you have never experienced it then you do not understand what it means. We have been able to travel to the South, and every time we encounter Southern hospitality we leave blown away by how special all guests are treated. Once my wife and I (Chris) took six of our children and my Grandma halfway across the country to North Carolina. When we arrived at my Aunt Irene's simple house in the small town of Goldsboro, she treated us as if royalty had shown up. At a restaurant serving amazing North Carolina-style barbecue, I went to grab the check, and my Aunt Irene slapped my hand while scolding me as if I had committed a mortal sin (my kids still laugh about this). At night, this same eighty-year-old woman slept in a recliner after insisting that we use her bed. WOW! We felt special and deeply moved by the love she poured upon us.

While hospitality certainly can be a natural virtue (a good habit we work at to acquire in which grace is not needed), it would seem like Southern hospitality is tied to a long Christian tradition and culture. As Catholics, it is also a part of our tradition. And elevated by grace, it should be a supernatural expression of the life of Christ in us.

St. Benedict and his order are shining examples of hospitality. His Rule states: "All guests of the monastery should be welcomed as Christ, because He will say, 'I was a stranger, and you took me in' (Mt 25:35). The greeting and farewell should be offered with great humility for with bowed head and a prostrate body all shall honor in the guest the person of Christ. For it is Christ who is really being received."[19] This is why, still to this day, when a Benedictine monastery is built it is required to have a guesthouse. Can each of us make our homes a guesthouse of Our Lord? Can we make sure that our churches are welcoming not only to Jesus in the tabernacle but to Jesus in the stranger?

We all know what happens at every Christmas and Easter Mass. We walk into the church on Christmas Eve or Easter morning to find the church packed, standing room only. There are people in our church who were not there last week, or last month, or perhaps this last year, and even worse they have the nerve to be sitting in *my* pew. This is an easy attitude to have, but we must change. We need to reach out to them, to welcome them and make them feel special. We need to make them feel like this is where they belong. We need to make them feel like they are famous because they are: the heavenly Father knows them by name.

This hospitality that we extend must be real and sincere. Hospitality that lacks sincerity is easy to see through. On an evening that I took my (Chris') oldest son to basketball practice at the YMCA, I was excited to get some time to work there on a talk about evangelization. I found a comfortable chair and took my notes and Bible out to settle in for the next hours. Two minutes later the man sitting beside me leaned over to ask, "So what are you doing?" A little annoyed, I simple answered, "I'm working on a talk," hoping that the answer would stop further questions. A minute later he leaned back in, "So are you a preacher?" As I quietly wondered why in the world I had to choose this seat I answered, "No, I'm a teacher, and I also go around the country to give talks." Surely that would be enough to stop the inquisition. But he followed up with, "So what do you talk about?" Frustrated, I was interiorly asking the Lord why I could not have just one hour with Him to work on this talk. I answered, "I speak about the need to share the Good News of salvation and train Catholics how to do that effectively." And then the scales fell from my eyes and the light shined into the darkness of my self-consumed heart. I put my Bible and notes away. We talked for about forty-five minutes. The conversation was good, but it remained pretty shallow. I cannot help but think that perhaps what prevented that conversation from going deeper was that he had picked up on my insincerity. I still pray for the man at the Y and hope that I can make up for my lack of hospitality.

Hospitality must be an attitude we instill in every parishioner. From the pastor to the volunteers, from the secretaries to the janitors. If strangers come to our church properties, then they must feel like they have come home.

In fact, our own family homes should be an extension of the parish church. Our Christian homes should be houses of hospitality, lights in the neighborhood.

Hospitality builds upon and is an extension of our invitation. Simple statements such as, "I'm glad you came," "Hope to see you again," "Do you have any questions," or "What did you think," will demonstrate that our invitation was sincere. When we, our parishes, and our homes become places of hospitality we will show others that they are welcome anytime and that this is where they belong. We will turn a stranger into a family member.

HOSPITABLE—The Practice

When Tony and I were speaking in New Orleans, we were walking the streets looking for an authentic crawfish boil. We were defeated and heading back to our hotel when we walked by a huge garage door open to the machine shop inside with a large number of people. As we were looking in a man asked us where we were from. I guess it was obvious we were outsiders. Tony answered, "We're from Kansas. What is all this?" With a thick Cajun accent he responded, "Oh, I'm just having a crawfish boil for all my employees."

I'm not sure if it was because of our wide eyes or the drool coming out of our mouths, but the local business owner said, "Why don't you come in and join us?" "Oh no, sir, we couldn't do that," I began. But the man said: "I insist. It will be the best crawfish boil you have ever had, I gerr-on-tee!" He brought us into the shop that held a canoe full of crawfish and all the "fixins." He gave each of us a beer and took the time to teach us how to eat the "mudbugs."

The Cajun ambassador made us feel as if he was waiting for us to show up. He served our needs before we could express them; he gave all of himself and his attention to us. It was an experience Tony and I will never forget. His hospitality was very Christ-like. He welcomed the strangers and made them feel as if they were home.

Our hospitality needs to be ***Honoring***, ***Humbling***, and ***Hyper-extensive***.

Hospitality is about bestowing ***Honor*** on the person who has come into our presence. Recall the story of the short tax collector named Zacchaeus, who longed to see Jesus but could not because of the large crowd (see Lk 19:1-10). Zacchaeus climbed a tree just to catch a glimpse of this prophet from Nazareth. The story took a dramatic turn when we find out that it was Jesus who was seeking Zacchaeus. The Lord said, "Make haste and come down; for I must stay at your house today" (Lk 19:6). Imagine how this made Zacchaeus feel. This welcome was so intense that it pushed Zacchaeus to change his life and amend all his wrongs.

Here's a contemporary example. My (Tony's) father had the extraordinary opportunity to meet Mother Teresa. On a trip to Calcutta, India, he was able to speak to her three different times. He said that when speaking with Mother Teresa she made him feel that he was the only one present to her and that she always had time, even though she was one of the busiest women in the world. She asked my father if he had any daughters, and he answered, "Yes." Mother Teresa said, "Then send me one to be a sister and work." My father responded, "Well, Mother, I have seven daughters." To which Mother quickly added, "Oh, then you can send me two." With her finger in his chest she said, "You have a fire in your heart, keep that burning."

Then Mother Teresa asked him if he would take back to America a baby who had a heart problem. My father, who always had an open-door policy to children in need, said he was willing but was concerned about the timing since he was leaving the next day. Mother assured him that she could get it done because she had power: "I have power, pray for me, pray that I do not abuse my power, because if I abuse it I will lose it."

A living saint asked my father for prayers. He said he would pray for her and asked Mother Teresa to pray for him and his family. (Seems like a good exchange.) My father was not able to bring back the baby, but that encounter with Mother Teresa lifted his spirits and blessed our entire family.

An authentic hospitality will bestow upon strangers honor, which will make them aware of the honor the Savior of the World wishes to restore to their dignity.

True hospitality is a ***Humbling*** act of service. When Jesus visited the house of a prominent Pharisee, the example of hospitality came from an unexpected visitor (see Lk 7:36-50). A women known to be a sinner washed Jesus' feet with her tears, wiped them with her hair, and anointed them with ointment. Jesus pointed out to the Pharisee: "Do you see this woman? I entered your house, you gave me no water for my feet, but she has wet my feet with her tears and wiped them with her hair. You gave me no kiss, but from the time I came in she has not ceased to kiss my feet. You did not anoint my head with oil, but she has anointed my feet with ointment." What did the woman get for her hospitality? The woman received more than could be imagined as Jesus said: "Your sins are forgiven.... Your faith has saved you; go in peace." We must see our hospitality as more than just a natural welcoming of a stranger, but as welcoming Jesus Christ himself so that our faith will be shown, forgiveness will be received, and peace will be given.

Members of the Benedictine order take their hospitality seriously because it is so clearly biblical. The Book of Hebrews says, "Do not neglect to show hospitality to strangers, for thereby some have entertained angels unawares" (13:2). In my (Tony's) last semester at Benedictine College I visited a monk who had become a close friend. I asked him if I could give him some money to buy me a large icon of St. Benedict the next time he went up to the abbey in Conception, Missouri. The monk turned around and grabbed his personal icon of St. Benedict hanging on the wall.

"No, Father," I said, "I don't want yours. I'm just asking if you are going up to the abbey sometime…" I refused his offer a few more times, but the monk's insistence won out. As I was walking away from his office I turned over the icon to see an inscription: "Congratulations on your ordination to the priesthood," with the date. Making a quick U-turn, I headed back to the office to give the icon back. Father said: "This Lent I made a commitment to give immediately whatever people ask of me. The icon is yours. I simply ask that you hang it near the entrance of your home to welcome all those that arrive." It hangs there to this day.

It is interesting that hospitality must be given with humility, and it also requires humility to receive it. It is hard to see sometimes, but to accept a gift requires humility. For me, to walk out of the monk's office with the icon took much effort.

My (Chris') boys had to help out at a 4-H fundraiser. Their job was to assist the customers out to their cars with their bags by asking, "Can I carry your bags out to the car?" One after another the customers would say, "No, thank you, I got it." This was actually taking the opportunity of service away from the boys. So my wife told them to ask, "Would you please *allow* me to carry your bags to the car?" They were able to serve a few more people than before.

Hospitality is about lowering ourselves even lower than those we want to serve. Through offering hospitality that is humbling, we can lift those up to enjoy the banquet of the Lord no matter how humble their background may be.

This kind of hospitality must be ***Hyper-extensive***—that is, it must extend over and above what is normal, and it must extend from all of us. St. Paul said: "I have become all things to all men, that I might by all means save some. I do it all for the sake of the gospel, that I may share in its blessings" (1 Cor 9:22-23). I remember a fellow religion teacher always asking me about the weekend's sports happenings. "Who won? Who lost? What did you think of that? Who do you think will win next weekend?" To most men these questions are a normal occurrence, but this particular religion teacher asking the questions had little to no interest in sports. It began to make sense once when I overheard his class. He was talking with the students about the weekend games and restating my opinions (as his own) about what would happen next weekend. While he had no interest in sports, his students did, and thus he became all things to his students. That is hyper-extensive hospitality. He knew if the students believed he cared about their interests, then perhaps they would care about what he wanted to teach them.

Our hospitality must extend to all people. Hospitality is not just for those who look like us or have our same interests. Both of our families are your average clean-cut Midwestern families who dress up to go to Sunday Mass. When people come to Mass not dressed in "Sunday Best," it becomes easy to judge them, but we must push beyond our natural reactions to reach a supernatural hospitality. We take our kids to the soup kitchens, family shelters, and special-needs camps in order to raise our children in a culture of hospitality. My (Chris') mother-in-law says, "There will be two regrets that we will have at the time of our judgment: why we didn't love God more and why we didn't love our neighbor more." So let's be sure to be hyper-extensive with our hospitality so that no one will ever feel excluded from the grace that Christ wishes to offer.

We have had people tell us, "Hospitality does not change people's lives, but grace and the Eucharist changes people's lives." We agree, but we do know that genuine hospitality can open people up to grace, and we are certain that we will be judged for the hospitality we extend: "Come, O blessed of my Father, inherit the kingdom prepared for you from the foundation of the world; for I was hungry and you gave me food, I was thirsty and you gave me drink, I was a stranger and you welcomed me" (Mt 25:34-35).

If we practice an authentic hospitality that is honoring, humbling, and hyper-extensive, we can hope that strangers will be inspired to hear the Good News that Christ has waiting for them.

Pillar 4

INSPIRATIONAL—The Principle

When I (Tony) was teaching high school seniors who lacked motivation and believed inspiration was impossible, I laid out a challenge to them: "I bet we can get your classmates excited about anything." So I chose something neutral.

"Have you heard of Tang? It's delicious. It has so many vitamins and so many different flavors. Neil Armstrong drank it on the moon! Let's get excited about Tang, start drinking it, and get others to drink it with us."

The students were in, except for one kid in the back who refused to participate … which was perfect. I told him: "Good, we have to have an antagonist. Otherwise it will seem fake."

The students began to bring Tang bottles and powder. I had to tell the local grocery-store manager to stock up on more Tang because he was running out. After two weeks of this activity I went through the cafeteria of the 1,200-student high school and secretly counted how many were drinking Tang: more than 50 percent.

After the experiment the students knew that inspiring their peers was possible, so I said: "How about now we try to inspire our peers to something that really matters? We inspire them to be saints."

The Gospels say that Jesus spoke differently. "The crowds were astonished at his teaching, for He taught them as one who had authority, and not as their scribes" (Mt 7:28-

29), and they declared that Jesus "had done all things well" (Mk 7:37). It was different not because of manner or method, but because Jesus' message had power. Jesus brought a teaching that offered a new hope and a new life. He was inspiring. Jesus' message changed the lives around Him and it changed the world. Do we really believe that the message we are sharing with others has the power to change lives and to continue to change our world today?

Between our words and our lives, the world must know that we are called to be something more than this life has to offer. There is a hunger in each person for happiness, but this hunger is insatiable. No matter how happy we are, we can always be happier.

On the day that my (Chris') first child was born I thought, "I couldn't imagine being any happier than I am right now." But if someone would have come into the room to announce to me, "Chris, you just won a million-dollar lottery," guess what, I would have been happier. And if someone told me I didn't have to pay taxes on it, I would be even happier.

This insatiable appetite will not be quenched on earth. It is an infinite desire to be happy. Only an infinite God can satisfy an unlimited desire. We are made for more than this world, we are made for God. In the words of St. Augustine: "You have made us for yourself, and our heart is restless until it rests in you."[20]

This insatiable appetite also creates some problems within us. Sometimes we try to satisfy the infinite desire with finite things, but this will never work. Anyone who has been around serious addictions usually ask themselves, "How does someone become addicted to (fill in the blank)." The answer lies within this insatiable appetite. We always will have this nagging feeling that "I could be happier." So we seek more of these finite goods until we become enslaved to those desires. This can play havoc on our marriages, because we want our spouses to make us happy like we long to be happy. But they cannot because even our spouses are finite. Pope Benedict XVI described this perfectly when he said, "The world offers you comfort, but you are not made for comfort, you were made for greatness."[21]

Remember what it was like to be young and daydream? I (Chris) remember hours spent in my backyard playing basketball. In my mind I would count down the seconds of the clock in order to take the last winning shot in the championship game. All of us dream of greatness, but perhaps reality, the world, and sin have beaten it out of us. The desire for greatness has been placed there by God. The Gospel message declares that God wants to restore us to our relationship with Him—namely, to be sons and daughters of the almighty King of the Universe.

There is an American attitude that says, "Good is not good enough." Meaning just "good" is not "enough" when it comes to business, athletics, academics, or money. A business makes its first million and begins to plan how to make its second. A team wins a championship and it begins immediate preparations on how it can repeat. Our TVs are bigger and clearer than they were forty years ago. Our video games today make old machines look like moving stick figures. When it comes to every part of our lives, we never settle for just "good."

However, when it comes to our spiritual lives, all of a sudden "good" becomes just fine. The problem is, Jesus Christ did not hang on the cross for three hours for us to be "good." He was not brutally scourged for us to be a "little different." Christ was not crowned with thorns just so we wouldn't get drunk, use drugs, or commit adultery. Quite frankly, common sense could tell us not to do those things.

The Savior of the World did not come to give us common sense; He came to give us grace. Jesus came so that we could live a life that was supernatural, unworldly, so that we could love our enemies and forgive those who persecute us. Jesus came to pull us out of the mud and the muck so that we can walk on water, so that we can move mountains. Jesus wants us to be nothing less than saints, to "be perfect as the heavenly Father is perfect" (Mt 5:48). That is a truly inspirational message. Are we ready to preach that message with our words and our lives? Do our lives bear witness to that truth?

It seems as if the Gospel many people are sharing with the world is that Jesus came so we can stop sinning. Indeed, the salvation Christ won for us on the cross was meant to pull us out of our sin and give us the ability to overcome temptations. But this is neither the entire story nor the most inspirational part of the story. Imagine a coach at the beginning of the season, in the first practice, delivering a passionate speech about how the goal for the season is to make sure the team does not finish last. That is not motivating. Instead, a coach is going to lift the players up and get them imagining accomplishments they never thought were possible. Jesus does exactly this for us. The grace He won for us allows us to go beyond our natural abilities to live supernatural lives.

Supernatural lives are what the world cannot ignore. Lives that are lived with such supernatural grace cause the world to stop and say, "Wow." This is what has happened with the lives of the saints for two thousand years. Their lives show us what the Gospel is actually capable of accomplishing in us. To return to the sports analogy, the lives of the saints are like championship banners hanging in the gym that show us what others before have done, and therefore we must shoot for the same way of life.

Our words and our lives, our marriages and our families, our way of doing business and our way of playing, our parishes and our dioceses, all must be vivid signs in this world that we are called to live supernaturally. We are called to be saints. This is a message worth getting out of bed in the morning for. This is a message worth sharing. This is a message that can inspire the world to return to the source of its greatness, the Triune God.

INSPIRATIONAL—The Practice

In the school where we teach, Kapaun Mt. Carmel Catholic High School, there hangs a four-foot wooden crucifix carved in honor of Father Emil Kapaun.[22] He was a priest of the Diocese of Wichita, Kansas, who became a U.S. Army chaplain. He spent that last seven months of his life in a POW concentration camp in North Korea and died a victim of malnutrition, harsh treatment, and pneumonia. During his service, and especially in the POW camp, he took care of "his boys" with a supernatural love. His faith was not shaken by the communist captors and served as a light in the darkness. His unimaginable selfless acts gave hope to the soldiers in a place and time in which there was none. A fellow captive said of Father Kapaun, "By his very presence, somehow, he could turn a stinking, louse-ridden, mud hut, for a little while, into a cathedral."[23]

Father Kapaun's life and death inspired that wooden crucifix. It was carved by Major Gerald Fink, a fellow POW. However, Major Fink, who was Jewish, never knew Father Kapaun personally, just through the stories the POWs told of the chaplain.

What could inspire men in a POW camp in such a way? Someone living ***Faith***, ***Hope***, and ***Love*** in an extraordinary manner during an extraordinary time. We live in an extraordinary time, and we must live inspirational lives. We will be able to effectively evangelize when our lives are inspirationally centered on ***Faith***, ***Hope***, and ***Love***.

We must be a people who are faithful, or in other words, full of ***Faith***. Those who have been married for years knows that to be faithful in marriage is not simply refraining from adulterous acts, but instead are giving completely of themselves to their spouses, in good times and bad, sickness and health, always and every day. Our faithfulness to the Lord must be the same way: entirely giving ourselves to Him, willing to step out of the boat.

There are two ways we use the word "faith" in our Catholic tradition. The first is what we could describe as a capital F "Faith." This is the teachings of the Church which we all share in common (which is summed up in the *Catechism of the Catholic Church*) and which we share with millions of brothers and sisters throughout the world and history. We must be loyal to these teachings. If those who we are trying to evangelize see any hypocrisy in us it will put a huge obstacle in their path to the Church. We must study the Faith more. In a marriage there will never be a time in which there is not something else one can learn about one's spouse. So, too, with the Faith; there is always more to learn. And the better we know the Faith, the more inspirational we can be in our evangelizing.

The second type of faith is what we can refer to as a lowercase f "faith." This is our personal adherence to the "Faith." It's the faith that expects God to answer our prayers. This faith, too, must grow stronger.

The first tip we have is to pray for more faith. God will always give us faith if we ask for it. However, we receive it only to the extent that we are open to the gift.

The second tip for growth in faith is to completely pour ourselves into the Faith. Take everything that the Church gives us and make it ours: liturgies, Scripture, tradition, and customs. St. Paul speaks of a living faith to the Galatians: "I have been crucified with Christ; it is no longer I who live, but Christ who lives in me; and the life I now live in the flesh I live by faith in the Son of God, who loved me and gave himself for me" (Gal 2:20). When we live the Faith our faith is sure to grow. When our faith is alive then the Faith will become so incredibly attractive to those around us, making our evangelization effective.

We currently live in a world that lacks ***Hope***. When we look around, it doesn't take long to see that people are searching for more than what this world has to offer.

"'Shawn" was a young man who I (Chris) had worked with in my high school youth group. It had been a long journey thus far, involving mini-conversion after mini-conversion, but some habits such as drug use and sexual activity die hard. After the summer he graduated, Shawn dropped off the face of the earth. A year had gone by when he walked into my office and through his tears told me how his sins where just too bad and had become repetitive to the point of habits. I stopped Shawn at that point and instructed him to follow me. We left my office, walked down to the empty church, and took a seat on the floor in front of the first pew.

I asked him to repeat what he had said to me in my office. He began, but I interrupted and said: "No, do not tell me that your sins are too bad or too many for Christ to forgive. Tell *Him*. Look at that crucifix and tell *Him* that *He* did not suffer enough for you. Tell *Him* that if He had only been scourged a few more times or hung on that cross for a few more minutes then perhaps He would have done enough to be able to forgive you of your sins." Silence. I simply stated the obvious: "It sounds silly doesn't it; well imagine how silly it must sound to Christ." There is no sin that Christ cannot forgive. Praise God, alleluia, alleluia! Shawn went to confession and through the grace of God turned his life around. He is now a police officer who is married and has a faith-filled family.

True hope has the ability to change us and the world around us. We have a true hope that is certain because Christ has saved us. The hope is certain because it has changed our lives. We are able to make different and better decisions with the grace of God than if we were not saved.

Pope Benedict XVI said, "The one who has hope lives differently; the one who hopes has been granted the gift of a new life."[24] Hope changes us, it changes everything it encounters, and it can change the world. The hope that Christ gives us must move out from us to the world, as Pope Francis has said: "In your heart you know that it is not the same to live without him; what you have come to realize, what has helped you to live and given you hope, is what you also need to communicate to others."[25]

With an increase in living out our Christian hope we will evangelize more inspirationally, thus this world will always have hope.

If we were to try to sum up the Gospel message in one word, it could only be ***Love***. Perhaps the most famous Bible verse and one that we should have memorized is, "For God so loved the world that he gave his only begotten Son, that whoever believes in him should not perish but have eternal life" (Jn 3:16). Of the theological virtues (faith, hope, and love), love is the greatest (see 1 Cor 13:13). Love is to be the supreme character marker by which all people will be able to recognize that we are followers of Christ (Jn 13:35). We are loved by God and were created to love.

In 1956, the television show *Alfred Hitchcock Presents* aired an episode called "The Legacy." In it, Hitchcock told an intriguing tale of a wealthy couple named Howard and Irene Cole. Initially, the husband spent all his time with younger, beautiful women—playing tennis, dining, and dancing with them. Even in middle of that scandal, Irene defended her husband and their marriage by saying that they loved each other, and that was just how their marriage was. She believed she was just not that interesting.

That was when Prince Burhan of India—a tall, dark, and handsome playboy—arrived on the scene and immediately took an interest in Irene. They spent all their time together. Dining, dancing, and picnicking, to the point that it created another scandal. Eventually, Prince Burhan told Irene that he loved her and begged her to leave her husband. She refused. Prince Burhan promised that if she did not come away with him then he would kill himself. Even so, Irene remained faithful to Howard. The next day Prince Burhan was found dead in a car accident which looked to be an apparent suicide.

In the final scene, Hitchcock presented to us a "new" Howard and Irene Cole. She is confident and beautiful. He never leaves her side. What was it that changed Irene and her marriage? It was this: she found herself loved by a prince; she was loved by someone that everyone else just dreamed to be in the presence of; she was loved by someone of whose love she believed she was not worthy of. Love changed her.

Here is the news flash, *GOD LOVES YOU!* And, *GOD'S LOVE WILL CHANGE YOU, TOO!* And, He is *much* more impressive than some prince.

What we must do is allow God's love to transform us. As Pope Francis has pointed out, we must receive God's love in order to be able to give love: "We become fully human when we become more than human, when we let God bring us beyond ourselves in order to attain the fullest truth of our being. Here we find the source and inspiration of all our efforts at evangelization. For if we have received the love which restores meaning to our lives, how can we fail to share that love with others?"[26] Once we are transformed and truly know that we are loved by God, we will then experience the uncontainable desire to tell others of the love of God and the transformation that His love can create in them.

Furthermore, God's love is so great that it is not enough to just talk about it with others. We are compelled to impart His love to others. The more we understand ourselves as beings loved by God, and the more we seek to love God, then the more our desire to share that love with others will grow. Pope Francis has stated, "An evangelizing community knows that the Lord has taken the initiative, he has loved us first (cf. 1 Jn 4:19), and therefore we can move forward, boldly take the initiative, go out to others, seek those who have fallen away, stand at the crossroads and welcome the outcast."[27]

Love changes everything. Love has the power to change this world.

If we desire our effective evangelization to be inspirational then we must be focused on these theological virtues. We must deepen our faith in order to be a sign of the Faith to others. When we live our new life in Christ it will give hope to this world drowning in despair. The more we grow in love with Jesus Christ the more we will love to bring His salvation to the lost and hurting.

Pillar 5

SACRAMENTAL—The Principle

Those of us who are "cradle Catholics" can usually recall memories of our first Communion: the three-piece suit or white dress, the family, celebration, gifts, and cake. Recall the anticipation and the excitement of finally being able to receive Our Lord in the Blessed Sacrament. For those who are converts to Catholicism, recall the Easter Vigil in which you entered the Church. Remember the nerves, the excitement, the wonder, and awe.

When I (Chris) was in college at Franciscan University in Steubenville, Ohio, the Easter Vigil was not only the pinnacle of the liturgical year, but it was the most exciting time of the school year. Students would line up an hour early for the Vigil service that lasted four hours. The music, passion, and preaching were enough to convince you that you were experiencing a slice of the worship in heaven.

I will never forget the moment that the catechumens officially entered the Church. The priest would baptize them in a small, shallow pool. When he finished the words, "and in the name of the Holy Spirit," the new Christian would come up soaking wet and the congregation would explode into applause and cheers as if their football team had just scored the winning touchdown. It was as if they had just witnessed a dead man walking out of a tomb—which is exactly what we witness at every baptism. The joy of that moment was enough to bring tears to many eyes. And that joy is what each of us should experience when we encounter the sacraments.

Jesus Christ came to redeem humanity, to be the Savior of the World. His mission was to reestablish a relationship between God and humanity. In order for that relationship to be restored, Christ won for us grace, and He decided that the grace would be delivered to us in the sacraments. We assume that God could have delivered sanctifying grace in many different ways, but He chose to do so in the sacraments through ordinary elements, such as bread, wine, water, and oil.

The principle that "you can't give what you don't have" must be applied to the sacraments. We must live a dynamically sacramental lifestyle. Attending Mass attentively and going to confession regularly is the beginning of effective evangelization. The more you go to daily Mass the more you will hunger for it and miss it on the days that you cannot attend. The more time you spend in adoration in front of the Blessed Sacrament the more you will long to return. The more you experience Christ in the sacraments the greater your desire will grow to bring others to Him in the same experience. As the Second Vatican Council stated, "For the liturgy, 'through which the work of our redemption is accomplished,' most of all in the divine sacrifice of the Eucharist, is the outstanding means whereby the faithful may express in their lives, and manifest to others, the mystery of Christ and the real nature of the true Church."[28]

The more we experience Christ in the sacraments the more we will desire to share Christ with others and the more effective we will be, most especially by being attached to the Eucharist. Dom Chautard declared, "The efficacy of an apostolate almost invariably corresponds to the degree of Eucharistic life acquired by a soul."[29] There is no doubt that this is why Blessed Teresa of Calcutta insisted that her sisters spend time in prayer before the tabernacle. Or why St. Louis IX, King of France, went to Mass more than seven hundred times a year. Or why Archbishop Fulton Sheen spent an hour of adoration every day for sixty years in order to do the type of evangelization for which he was so famous.

Chautard goes on to describe this connection:

> When a preacher or catechist retains in himself the warm life of the Precious Blood, when his heart is consumed with the fire that consumes the Eucharistic Heart of Jesus, what life his words will have: they will burn, they will be living flames! And what effects the Eucharist will have, radiating throughout a class for instance, or through a hospital ward, or in a club, and so on, when the ones God has chosen to work there have nourished their zeal in holy Communion, and have become *Christ-bearers*![30]

Interiorizing the grace of the Eucharist, as Chautard observes, makes us like the Mother of God, the *Theotokos* (God-Bearer). Mary bearing Christ in her body brought the Savior to her kinswoman Elizabeth and ultimately to all of mankind. This must be our endeavor as well: to receive Christ in our heart, in our intellect, and in our will, in order to bring Him to everyone we encounter.

As the desire to evangelize grows we come to realize that we cannot give people what they really need. Only Christ can give them the grace that they need. Christ and His grace are in the sacraments, and, therefore, evangelization and sacraments go hand in hand. The *Catechism* states: "Christ sent his apostles so that 'repentance and forgiveness of sins should be preached in his name to all nations' (Lk 24:47). 'Go therefore and make disciples of all nations, baptizing them in the name of the Father and of the Son and of the Holy Spirit' (Mt 28:19). The mission to baptize, and so the sacramental mission, is implied in the mission to evangelize, because the sacrament is prepared for by the word of God and by the faith which is assent to this word" (*CCC*, 1122). Our job is not to impose Christ and the sacraments on people but to simply propose.

Authors Ralph Martin and Peter Williamson describe our role as ushers. "True evangelization is like being an usher at a theater. An *usher* brings people in, sits them down and facilitates their watching the play. The central figure in the play is Jesus Christ. If I think of myself as the *major actor* in that play, I will not let the Christ in me evangelize those I am trying to serve."[31] This is no more evident than in our attempts to get others to the sacraments. We must be willing to lead, to encourage, and to "usher" (even if that literally means driving) others to the sacraments.

I (Chris) learned this lesson of being an usher for evangelization when it was my job to give a "confession prep" talk to a group of high school students. This is not a particularly fun talk to give, because the point of it is to convince everyone that they are sinners and need to go to confession. While I was giving the talk there was a young man in the back corner who was having none of it. His physical posture demonstrated no interest. He would not make eye contact with me except for twice, and I took that as a bodily threat.

When the talk was over we took the youth over to the church. The Eucharist was exposed in adoration and the priest went into the confessional. That young man was the first to follow the priest in. He came out, knelt down for just a little bit, and then came over to me. He asked me if I had something with the Hail Mary on it. I found a card for him and he knelt there in front of Our Lord for the entire hour. At the end of the night the young man came up to me to shake my hand and said, "Thank you." He turned around and walked home. I know that there was nothing that I said or did for him because I saw his physical natural reaction. But I did put him in a position where he could encounter the Living Almighty Merciful God in the sacrament of confession.

This is why we should try to make the sacraments available at every parish event, whether it is a mission, retreat, conference, or even a picnic. Open up the event with Mass or close it with Adoration and Benediction. And we should try to find a way to make confession available at some point. If it is just a small group, do the Liturgy of the Hours. By putting people into contact with the sacraments and liturgies of the Church we let them see and taste a piece of heaven. We cannot give what we do not have, but the sacraments give everyone what they truly need, which is grace, and the Holy Spirit has that responsibility.

In this work of evangelization we realize that the sacraments have a threefold purpose: they are for ***you***, for ***us***, and for ***them***.

The sacraments are meant for ***you*** to encounter the person of Jesus Christ individually. We have to be a people steeped in the sacramental experience. We have yet to meet someone who started making an effort to go to Mass more than once a week who did not notice a profound impact in their faith life.

Obviously, there is the precept of the Church that requires confession once a year, but we highly encourage a habitual reception of the sacrament. If it is a matter of mortal sin, then go immediately. Knock on a rectory door if you have to. It will not be the first time that has happened.

We suggest the habit of at least once a month. Associate it to something in your normal routine. For me (Chris), I get a haircut once a month. So when I get a haircut I also know it's time to go to confession. "Make my hair look good, make my soul look good" is an easy connection.

If you begin to go to Mass more often, go to confession at least once a month, and if your life is not somehow better in six months then please email me at chris@CastingNetsOnline.com and I will personally send you a refund for this book.

The sacraments change ***us***. Imagine a parish where Mass attendance on Tuesday is 75 percent of Mass attendance on Sunday. Imagine a parish where the confession line is as long as the Communion line. The sacraments unite us as one body. The sacraments bring us closer to one another. If Jesus was standing in front of us and we took a step closer to Him, we have stepped closer to God and man, because that is what He is. And if we are all in a circle stepping closer to Jesus, then we are all also stepping closer to one another.

Going to confession will give us more patience with our neighbors and we will be more quickly able to forgive our family. If we have just received Our Lord in the Eucharist, then hopefully the love the Savior has for us will flow out to others. The sacraments bind us together, and they will continue to make that bond stronger. "The bread which we break, is it not a participation in the body of Christ? Because there is one bread, we who are many are one body, for we all partake of the one bread" (1 Cor 10:16-17).

The sacraments are meant for ***them***—that is, for those who are not yet in the Church. In the work of evangelization what are we inviting people to? Or welcoming them to? Or ushering them to? Ultimately, it is to bring them to the sacraments.

The *Catechism* makes clear this connection between evangelization and the sacraments when it says:

> The Church affirms that for believers the sacraments of the New Covenant are *necessary for salvation.* "Sacramental grace" is the grace of the Holy Spirit, given by Christ and proper to each sacrament. The Spirit heals and transforms those who receive him by conforming them to the Son of God. The fruit of the sacramental life is that the Spirit of adoption makes the faithful partakers in the divine nature by uniting them in a living union with the only Son, the Savior. (1129, emphasis in original)

The sacraments will change you, and therefore it will change us, which will more effectively bring them—bring others—to the Font of Eternal Life.

SACRAMENTAL—The Practice

When my (Tony's) oldest daughter made her first Communion, it was a very exciting time for our family. And like most things in my life I go big. We invited family and friends over to rejoice with us.

We even invited our non-Catholic neighbors to the reception. "Come on over. We are going to have plenty of food and cake. Please come and celebrate with us." I was happy when they actually showed up. In the midst of the party my neighbor asked me, "So why is your daughter dressed up like a bride?" Inside I was laughing at the thoughts of what this weird custom could be leading my neighbor to conjure up. I explained to him the Catholic teaching on baptism, purity, and the Eucharist. I am sure he was more comfortable at the party now knowing that we were not trying to marry off our seven-year-old daughter.

All seven sacraments play a role in evangelization. However, we want to focus on four of them that play the largest role in evangelization or giving us opportunities to extend the Kingdom: ***Baptism***, ***Confirmation***, ***Eucharist,*** and ***Confession***.

Baptism is known as the "gateway sacrament." It gains us access to the other sacraments. We have noticed that among Catholics there has been a loss of understanding of this all-important sacrament. We need to recapture the truth that baptism is urgent and necessary. The *Catechism of the Catholic Church* could not declare any more boldly:

> The Lord himself affirms that Baptism is necessary for salvation. He also commands his disciples to proclaim the Gospel to all nations and to baptize them.

> Baptism is necessary for salvation for those to whom the Gospel has been proclaimed and who have had the possibility of asking for this sacrament. The Church does not know of any means other than Baptism that assures entry into eternal beatitude; this is why she takes care not to neglect the mission she has received from the Lord to see that all who can be baptized are "reborn of water and the Spirit." *God has bound salvation to the sacrament of Baptism, but he himself is not bound by his sacraments.* (1257, emphasis in original)

This statement lays squarely on our hearts the absolute urgency of baptism. Is it *possible* to reach heaven without the rebirth of baptism? Maybe. Is it *possible* to pass the freshman college biology class without ever showing up to class? Maybe. But why would we leave up to a *possibility* something that is as important as eternal life. We need to encourage our family and friends to have their children baptized. We need to encourage our family and friends to enter RCIA this year. Do not wait anymore!

Obviously, we are always concerned with the thin line between "inviting" our loved ones to the sacraments and "nagging" them. Continue to invite with charity. Perhaps we just have to think of different and creative ways to keep asking. My (Chris') wife has written several "St. Nicholas Notes" to friends and family on St. Nicholas' feast day of December 6. They get a handwritten letter from St. Nicholas "himself," inviting them to join the Church this year. We know a pastor who every year sends a handwritten letter to non-Catholic spouses of parishioners inviting them to join the RCIA. Keep asking and keep thinking of new ways to bring people to baptism.

The Sacrament of Baptism is also a great opportunity to evangelize. You may normally invite immediate family and close friends to your baptism celebrations, but why not invite some co-workers and neighbors? Let the priest or deacon know that there might be some non-Catholics at the baptism and so time can be taken to explain what is happening and about the beauty of the liturgy.

Many parishes have a "baptism class" requirement before having their children baptized. What are we doing with these baptism classes? Many of these classes are filled with parents who do not regularly attend Sunday Mass. This is a crucial moment. We encourage parishes to put some of their best, most dynamic couples as instructors in these classes because the next time we see these parents it might be at their child's first Communion. Encourage families to celebrate baptismal anniversaries as if they are birthdays. My (Chris') family allows our kids to pick the dinner meal for their special day. We have angel food cake and ice cream, and we light their baptismal candle while singing to them "Happy Baptism Day." Godparents should call or write their godchildren on their baptismal day. These little customs can make such an impression upon our children.

The Sacrament of ***Confirmation*** invokes so many different memories and realities for different Catholics that it can be a very confusing sacrament. Confirmation is a sacrament of initiation. It is not a "confirming" of our adult faith, but instead is a deepening of the graces of baptism. This is why even infants can receive confirmation. We must recapture the understanding of the power of Jesus Christ and the Holy Spirit instead of emphasizing the individual's acceptance of the Faith.

Many young people leave the Faith after they have been confirmed. Why? We believe that it is a horrible sign that even though the confirmandi (those being confirmed) have been baptized they have not been evangelized. Parishes must commit disciples with a heart for youths, for the lost and broken, into our confirmation programs. The confirmation classes cannot be just about intellectual catechesis but must be a real encounter with Jesus. We need leaders who are not just willing to meet with a small group of confirmandi but are willing to seek out one-on-one time with them. These need to be intentional disciples who are willing to be invested in the confirmandis' lives. Disciples who are willing to open their hearts up even if it means that their hearts gets broken. Without such women and men leading the confirmation classes, it will not matter what "program" or materials a parish uses—their young people will continue to walk away.

We must meet with the confirmation sponsors the confirmandi have chosen, both as an opportunity to call the sponsors to a deeper relationship to Christ and also to discuss the weight of their responsibilities. All too often the role of confirmation sponsor is just a title or merely seen as an honor. We need to teach the sponsors that their role is necessary, involved, important, and irreplaceable. The sponsor must encourage and support the confirmandi in renewing their commitment to living their baptismal promises.

The holy ***Eucharist*** is the center of our faith. As the *Catechism* says:

> The Eucharist is "the source and summit of the Christian life." "The other sacraments, and indeed all ecclesiastical ministries and works of the apostolate, are bound up with the Eucharist and are oriented toward

> it. For in the blessed Eucharist is contained the whole spiritual good of the Church, namely Christ himself, our Pasch." (1324)

This should be the real reason why we are sharing our faith.

Pope Francis said:

> How good it is to stand before a crucifix, or on our knees before the Blessed Sacrament, and simply to be in his presence! How much good it does us when he once more touches our lives and impels us to share his new life! What then happens is that "we speak of what we have seen and heard" (1 Jn 1:3).[32]

The Eucharist has so much to teach us about evangelization, such as the humility of God. God is willing to approach us not just simply as a human but in the form of bread and wine. Our Lord is willing to be gnawed, swallowed, dropped, or spilled in order to commune with us, to be one with us. Our Lord is willing to get messy just to have a closer relationship with us. Are we willing to get messy in order for others to commune with Christ? Are we willing to humble ourselves to serve them? In John's Gospel, the Eucharistic narrative is replaced with the account of Jesus washing the apostles' feet. He gives them the Eucharist, but He also shows them what the Eucharist looks like in serving one another. Can we do the same?

Confession is the sacrament of the New Evangelization. Any place we have gone where effective evangelization is taking place we have seen confession be a central part of the fruit. Cardinal Timothy Dolan describes why: "The Sacrament of Reconciliation *evangelizes the evangelizers*, as it brings us sacramentally into contact with Jesus, who calls us to conversion of heart, and allows us to answer his invitation to repentance—a repentance from within that can then transform the world without."[33]

We must be a constant symbol to our children, grandchildren, neighbors, co-workers, and the world that the mercy of God is always available if we but turn to Him. And we can do this by going to confession regularly. Pope Francis begged for our parishes to make this happen:

> I want to remind priests that the confessional must not be a torture chamber but rather an encounter with the Lord's mercy which spurs us on to do our best. A small step, in the midst of great human limitations, can be more pleasing to God than a life which appears outwardly in order but moves through the day without confronting great difficulties. Everyone needs to be touched by the comfort and attraction of God's saving love, which is mysteriously at work in each person, above and beyond their faults and failings.[34]

Our parishes must have the sacrament of confession available consistently and often for the New Evangelization to bring in the catch Our Lord desires.

The more we approach this sacrament of forgiveness the more effective we will be in encouraging others to do the same. We must share the beauty of what confession does for us. It is much like going to a doctor, which may not be our favorite activity. But when we have a good doctor who can bring us to health we walk away from the doctor's office with gratitude for his skills. And we tell others about the talents of our doctor.

Of course, we might feel shame in going to confession or we might beat ourselves up for falling into the same sins over and over. But as Pope Francis says about the greatness of confession:

> Do not be afraid of confession! When one is in line to go to confession, one feels all these things, even shame, but then when one finishes confession one leaves free, grand, beautiful, forgiven, candid, happy. This is the beauty of confession! ... Dear friends, celebrating the Sacrament of Reconciliation means being enfolded in a warm embrace: it is the embrace of the Father's infinite mercy.[35]

Let's tell others about this beauty.

We are sharing Jesus Christ when we evangelize. Therefore, we can say that the sacraments are the reason we evangelize, since it is Jesus we meet and encounter in the sacraments. We must be evangelizers that are centered on the sacraments so that we can effectively usher people to them as well. The process will continue throughout our lives and only grow deeper in our efforts to share the Faith.

Pillar 6

FORMATIONAL—The Principle

I (Chris) remember the first time I saw my wife. It was at a dance at Franciscan University. I can remember the first time I said, "I love you, Maria." It was in Christ the King chapel on the right side of the church in the third pew. I also remember telling her "I love you" on August 14, 1999, in Holy Family Cathedral in Orange, California. There were many people there, and we were in the front of the church, more dressed up than usual. I can usually also recall the last time I told Maria that I loved her because we have a relationship.

I cannot recall when I first learned what Maria's parents and siblings names were, where she went to high school, her favorite color, her favorite band, or her favorite movie, and yet I know all those things about Maria. You do not learn about the other person by going to a class or reading books but by living in the relationship with them.

And we must also think about formation in the Faith relationally. Do we really understand formation as an ongoing part of the conversion process? Or do we think of formation as something that we already did and can scratch it off the to-do list? Do we think of conversion as a process, or do we believe that conversion is something that happened in the past? Conversion is not a one-time event; it is a lifelong process (see *CCC*, 1427-1429). While we can point to a date in history on which we were baptized or the day we chose to live our faith, our life in Christ ought to be moving forward. There will never be a time when we are finished growing in the Faith.

Returning to the marriage example: There was one day (a very important day) that can be pointed to as the wedding. But any married couple can witness to the fact that the real work happens in the everyday relationship. After fifteen years of marriage, I (Chris) can say I know Maria better than I did fifteen years ago. Now, if someone would have asked me on our wedding day if I knew Maria, my answer would have been a quick and confident, "Yes, go ahead and test me, ask me anything about her." But today I can say I really do "know" her, not just facts about her, but I "know her." I expect that I will know Maria better in another fifteen years and even better in another thirty-five. If this is true for a finite person like my wife, then how much more true is it for an infinite person like God himself? When it comes to our faith there is always something more that we can know. Therefore, to continue daily conversion, formation must be ongoing.

To be effective in the work of evangelization we need to know that the work is never done. Conversion is not complete in us and is not complete in those we are ministering to. If we have a family member or friend come back to the Church, or enter the Church at Easter, we cannot clap our hands together and think, "We did it." No, the work is continuing. We must continue to help them become disciples who will go out and effectively evangelize.

The formation process is like trying to get into shape. Does a person go into a gym and lift two hundred pounds on the bench press one time, so they stay healthy? No, that is not how it works. Instead, we must go to the gym often and do repetitions of different workouts. The exercise must be part of a regular daily routine. We have to change our eating habits and make sure we are taking in the correct nutrition and vitamins. Then we will be on our way to a healthy life and lifestyle.

Our efforts of conversion and evangelization work the same way. Going to confession once, making a retreat once, or giving to the poor once will not make us holy. To the contrary, faith formation involves the continuous process of learning Catholic teaching and the disciplines that define us as Catholics. (More about this in the next chapter.)

We have met many good Catholics whose spirituality lives from one retreat or conference to the next—or, in other words, from one spiritual high to the next. They get excited at the event and then a few weeks later they slide into the same spiritual ruts and sins. This cannot be our way of living the Christian life. Now, certainly, there are highs and lows to any relationship, but the commitment to that relationship is a daily decision. And if this is true for us as we live the Catholic faith, then we also need to be aware of this tendency in those we are trying to bring to the Faith.

Continuing the comparison to marriage, formation and conversion must be a matter of the heart, mind, *and* will. When we first "fall in love," many times our emotions are leading the way. But if our mind does not come to know the beloved, then the emotions will not be enough to sustain us through difficult times. It is then that the will makes the decision to push through the difficult times and continue to love. The relationship with Christ must be shaped by love *and* knowledge. One without the other will not last. The relationship with Christ must be a matter of the heart, mind, and will.

If you came to the Church as adults you might recall that moment when you first realized the truth of Christ. Maybe with a powerful flood of emotion your life changed in an instant. Those (such as Tony and Chris) who left the practice of the Catholic faith for a time may remember that emotional moment of coming back into the arms of the Church. Even if you have been faithfully Catholic all your life, you probably recall moments that energized your faith. Maybe there was a really good homily, visit to the adoration chapel, retreat, mission, or conference in which you left feeling on cloud nine—that is, "feeling" God's personal love and mercy. In our Catholic tradition we call such experiences "consolations." These are little "booster shots" that God gives us as gifts to encourage us in our faith. We need to be aware of this in those who we are trying to evangelize. Give them opportunities to "fall in love" with Our Lord with beautiful churches, moving liturgies, powerful retreats, silent adoration, or meaningful personal conversations. However, like in our human relationships, it must be more than just emotions. It must move deeper.

In a marriage a growing knowledge of the beloved leads us to discovering how great our spouse truly is, which in turn strengthens the relationship. Our relationship with Christ will follow this same pattern. Knowing truly who Jesus is, the sacrifice He made for us, and how much He loves us pushes us through the difficult times in which we do not have consolations. Blessed Teresa of Calcutta shared that she went more than thirty years without experiencing any consolation in her spiritual life. What allowed her to accomplish all that she did was the certain knowledge of who Jesus was. And she knew that Jesus wanted her to love the poorest of the poor. For those who we are evangelizing, this means we must also make a priority of their catechetical formation because emotions will not sustain them.

However, as in our human relationships, one more component is needed: love, which is not an emotion or knowledge but a decision. In our human relationships emotions come and go, knowledge grows, but there are times when the will must act and make decisions. As men we have to make the decision to get over our fears and ask our beloved out; we have to save up our money and once again get over our fears to ask our beloved to marry us. As women you have to get over our corny pickup lines to say yes to going out. When he proposes, you have to trust that he is the one to spend the rest of your life with. Even after the wedding, every day you must make decisions to love: to take the trash out, mow the yard, change a dirty diaper, do the dishes, fold the laundry, or take the kids to practice—one decision of love after another.

Ultimately, a relationship with Christ also comes down to a decision—not simply a one-time choice, but a day-after-day decision to pick up our cross and follow Him. We need to encourage those we are evangelizing to make this choice. We cannot make it for them. It is between them and the Holy Spirit. We need to make sure that they know that this decision is not easy but it is worth it. It will involve carrying their cross and little daily deaths, but it will also bring with it a glorious resurrection.

FORMATIONAL—The Practice

At the encouragement of my (Tony's) wife, I decided it was the appropriate time to build a new deck on the back of our house. So I made the prudent decision to invite some of the high school guys I was teaching over to help me. This may not be the best idea if you are overly concerned about straight boards and ninety-degree angles. But I wanted to be able to spend some time outside of the classroom with the young men I had been teaching on a daily basis. I promised them a good time and to pay them with pizza for lunch and bratwursts for dinner. It was a normal construction project, but the day allowed me to begin some personal conversations with the guys.

Toward the later part of the day, one young man talked to me about his relationship with his girlfriend. I encouraged him to examine whether he was the man of God that he desired to be in his own heart in order to treat her like she should be treated. He felt that he was not close to that yet, so I said, "Well, then, you know what you need to do." The young man broke up with her and is now in his third year of theology as a diocesan seminarian. This simple moment of human relationship turned into meaningful formation.

Beneficial formation will always be in two components, to teach and to form. To teach is catechesis: the how, where, why, and what of our faith. Whether we are eight, eighteen, or ninety-eight, there is always something more we can know about our faith. Formation then is being trained in living the Christian life. What do the virtues look like in real life? How do we pray? What does it mean to forgive? What are our Christian duties in this world? To teach and to form, to teach and to form, and then to teach and to form. This should be an ever present cycle. As a model for formation, let's consider how Jesus did it.

How did Jesus spend His time during His public ministry? When we think of Jesus' public ministry the miracles are most often the first things to come to mind. However, Jesus spent more time teaching and forming people than He did physically healing them. The methods of Jesus' teaching and forming were as diverse as the miracles. When we think of Jesus teaching we immediately get into our minds images of Him preaching to the crowds like the Sermon on the Mount (see Mt 5-7), with many people around Him.

Yes, of course, He taught the masses, but He also spent time with individuals. Jesus had seventy-two disciples and from them He chose the Twelve Apostles. Within the Twelve there were three (Peter, James, and John) who received special formation. Even within the three Jesus singled out Peter for a special role. We love to imagine what those moments with Jesus that are not recorded in the Gospels must have been like. What must have been said during those long walks from town to town? What questions did the apostles ask the Son of God late at night when they were sitting around the campfire?

Many times I (Chris) notice that I teach certain things like my professors taught me, sometimes with the same gestures and mannerisms. We wonder, did John ever watch Peter preach and think to himself, "That was just how Jesus used to do it?" The overwhelming majority of formation that Jesus put into the apostles and disciples was not recorded in the Gospels. In fact, John says, "But there are also many other things which Jesus did; were every one of them to be written, I suppose that the world itself could not contain the books that would be written. (Jn 21:25).

Our formation must be just as diverse and constant; our formation must be ***Formal*** and ***Informal***.

Formal formation occurs in the normal catechetical instruction that happens in schools and parishes around the world on a weekly basis. It is the traditional classroom setting: parish school of religion, Catholic schools, RCIA, adult education, or parish missions that are used to instruct the faithful.

Contrary to popular opinion, catechesis' main target audience is adults and not children. If all of our adults were catechized it would certainly follow that there would be more catechized children. The bishops who gathered in 2012 for the Synod on the New Evangelization declared: "One cannot speak of the New Evangelization if the catechesis of adults is nonexistent, fragmented, weak or neglected. When these defects are present, pastoral ministry faces a very serious challenge."[36] By putting all of our focus and resources toward catechesis of children we are instilling the attitude that formation and conversion was a moment in the past instead of an unending, ongoing lifetime process.

About four years into my (Chris') teaching career, I realized that no matter how much passion I have or how great my methods are my catechesis will fall on deaf ears if the students in front of me are not first evangelized. For those who have or are doing formal catechesis, this is what we call "beating our head against a brick wall." St. John Paul II must have had this same experience:

> But in catechetical practice, this model order must allow for the fact that the initial evangelization has often not taken place.... This means that "cateche-

> sis" must often concern itself not only with nourishing and teaching the faith, but also with arousing it unceasingly with the help of grace, with opening the heart, with *converting*, and with preparing total adherence to Jesus Christ on the part of those who are still on the threshold of faith. This concern will in part decide the tone, the language, and the method of catechesis.[37]

Thus by putting catechesis in its proper place as one ongoing part of the lifelong process of evangelization, we can form disciples who will live the Gospel message dynamically. They will be able to communicate the joy of the Good News with all they will encounter.

Informal formation will never replace formal catechesis, but it is a necessary addition to those efforts. We receive and give informal formation on what it means to be a Christian in today's world simply through our personal relationships. The beautiful thing about this kind of formation is that it does not necessarily take more time. If we are going to build a deck, why not invite some people over to see how a Catholic builds a deck? If our family is going to watch a football game, why not invite over another family so they can see how a Catholic family watches a football game? We have to eat, so why not take someone out to breakfast or lunch once a week? As much as the apostles learned from hearing the Sermon on the Mount, we would be willing to bet that they learned as much, if not more, from eating, walking, and just spending time with Jesus.

In the first seven years of doing our radio show, we selected our high school students to be volunteer "producers." The student got the exciting job of running the sound board during the recording of the show. We have had eleven interns so far, and seven of them have gone into the seminary. Of the four who have not, one is still in high school and one is a girl, so she cannot. Why is this happening? We are not asking these young men every week, "When are you going to go into the seminary?" In fact, we are tired of needing to train new producers because the vocation director took another one. In all seriousness though, week after week our "interns" get to hear about the challenges of living our faith and communicating the Faith to the world. Week after week we get to build relationships with them. Week after week they get to ask questions in a non-threatening setting. Sure, when we eat, many times we talk about sports or trivial topics, but other times we get to discuss things that really do matter, and it is those conversations that can change eternity.

Bible studies are a great example of a mix between formal and informal formation. Normally they offer time for both personal interaction and community building. We need more family-to-family formation, older couples that reach out to younger couples. We need more one-on-one time with individuals either interested in Catholicism or are new to the Church. If we can match up our formal catechesis with some informal formation, then we will begin to produce disciples who are ready to be sent out on a mission to produce even more disciples like them.

Pillar 7

MISSIONFUL—The Principle[38]

I (Chris) can still remember the first week of teaching the Totus Tuus summer catechetical program. It was the summer of 1996, and it was the first time I was a part of a formal effort to evangelize. The excitement of trying to save the world one soul at a time was enough for us young adults to operate on just a few hours of sleep a night. When we were teaching we could not wait to get to our next prayer time. And when we were in prayer we could not wait to be able to talk to the young people we were evangelizing. It was a powerful week. I am still friends with some of the families I met that week. As the summer came to a close, I knew there was no going back to my former way of life. I had tasted the Living Water and more importantly the Lord had used me to bring others to that same Living Water. Like a child who had tasted a sweet dessert for the first time, I wanted more.

The Trinity is a communion of Persons that continually sends love out and has love return with more—more love and more communion. The Trinitarian God is full of mission, which we can see in Jesus' commission: "As the Father has sent me, even so I send you" (Jn 20:21). Therefore, we must be "missionful"—that is, full of mission. Those people who we have prayed about, invited, cared for, inspired, brought to the sacraments, and formed, must now turn outward. They, too, must be sent out with *The Seven Pillars* as their foundation to share this love and communion with others.

Any business must always be looking for ways to grow and expand, otherwise stagnation will set in and decline will not be far off. A good business will always be looking at how it can acquire the next customer or improve its product. Great businesses will be thinking of how they will be able to make their current customers happier and what they can do to stay one step ahead of their competitors. The Church is also like this.

The Church needs to be always looking outward to invite others to follow Christ. By her nature the Church is missionary. As Pope Paul VI said: "Evangelizing is in fact the grace and vocation proper to the Church, her deepest identity. She exists in order to evangelize, that is to say, in order to preach and teach, to be the channel of the gift of grace, to reconcile sinners with God, and to perpetuate Christ's sacrifice in the Mass, which is the memorial of His death and glorious resurrection."[39] If we are not reaching out we are not fulfilling the very reason that the Church exists.

The impact of a missionary attitude among the Church's members is incalculable. There are the tangible benefits of evangelization, such as more members and pews being filled. Full pews would bring economic growth for our parishes. Economic growth would allow us to build bigger churches and more infrastructure to create outreach programs to help those in need, both materially and spiritually. The confession lines would grow. We would be opening parishes and Catholic schools instead of closing them. Our seminaries could be full with young men who are faithful and zealous to serve the Bride of Christ.

Then there are the more important intangible benefits of evangelization, such as the salvation of souls. Evangelization proposes the life-changing message of the Good News to the world. Evangelization brings real hope to a culture drowning in despair. Evangelization overcomes the culture of death with the abundant life of Christ. Those are some pretty worthy reasons to evangelize, but there is more.

Evangelization also affects the evangelizer. Ask anyone who has been an RCIA sponsor or has participated in someone's conversion to Christ, "How did that affect your own faith?" Normally, they will respond that they felt they got more out of the process than the person they were sponsoring. It strengthens our faith to give the Faith away. As the Thirteenth Ordinary Synod of Bishops (2012) wrote: "Being Christian and 'being Church' means being missionary; one is or is not. Loving one's faith implies bearing witness to it, bringing it to others and allowing others to participate in it. The lack of missionary zeal is a lack of zeal for the Faith. On the contrary, faith is made stronger by transmitting it."[40] If we really want to do something to grow our faith, then we should share it with others.

My wife and I (Chris) have always loved inviting people of different faith traditions into our house to talk. Obviously, one of the most open faith traditions to enter our house has been members of the Church of Jesus Christ of Latter-day Saints (the Mormons). We have befriended about eight different sets of LDS missionaries. We got so close to one set of missionaries that I actually attended their three-hour Sunday service. During the second hour of the service, they divided everyone into what could be described as "Sunday school class" or a "catechism class." I was placed in the "beginner's class"; I guess my graduate degree in theology did not impress them.

The group included just the instructor, the two LDS missionaries, myself, and a woman who could be described as middle-aged and socially awkward. During the class I could not help but ask myself, "Why was she there?" Was she there because she found the doctrines of the church of LDS that convincing? I doubted it. I believe she was there because a couple of young men stopped by her house to show they cared.

The next question I asked myself was, "Where were the Catholics in her life?" One out of every three people on the west side of Wichita is Catholic. Percentages being what they are, a Catholic family lived within three doors of her. But she was not sitting at a Catholic parish. Perhaps no Catholics reached out to her to show her that she was loved. Since that experience, anytime I have a situation in which I am deliberating whether to speak about the Faith or not, I always think of her, and I reach out.

I was very impressed with the two-year LDS mission commitment of the young men I met. About 90 percent of all men undertake the two-year mission and about 60 percent of women do an eighteen-month mission. The Latter-day Saints is the fastest growing religion in the United States. While much credit can be given to their morally conservative beliefs, their pro-family stance, their closely knit communities, or their success in the secular world, I suggest that their "missionary program" has been the greatest source of their growth. If we want those whom we have helped to bring others to the Catholic Church, then we need to give them a missionful heart. Spreading the Good News will fill their hearts with a joy that is secure.

St. John Paul II many times spoke of a "springtime of evangelization." He believed that the New Evangelization would usher in a renewal of faith in the twenty-first century. If we become people of prayer, invite those we encounter, welcome and care for those who arrive on our doorsteps, deliver a message with our lives and lips that is inspiring, usher people to the sacraments, continually teach and form them, and then send them out to do the same, then we will have laid a firm foundation for a new outpouring of the Holy Spirit. This is not a task for the weak of heart, and it will not be easy. However, when Our Lord asks us to cast our nets out into the deep, will we be ready and willing to answer: "Master, we toiled all night and took nothing! But at your word I will let down the nets" (Lk 5:5)?

MISSIONFUL—The Practice

There are so many life lessons to be learned from marriage. We have already used marriage as a comparison to our relationship to Jesus Christ, but there is also a comparison that can be made between marriage and our work of evangelization.

In my (Chris') marriage there are things that I try to do daily. Every day I tell Maria, "I love you" and "You look beautiful today." No matter how busy we get, every day we talk, even if the dialogue is brief. ("How was your day?") Finally, we are always deciding to take our relationship deeper. We have even taken formal dance lessons to try a new activity together.

We must act the same way in our sharing the Faith. If we are going to be missionful and effective in our evangelization, then we must be committed to sharing the Gospel ***Daily***, looking for opportunities for ***Dialogue***, and taking people ***Deeper*** toward a relationship with Christ.

Evangelization must be something we are looking to do on a ***Daily*** basis, not just an activity we partake in here and there. Every morning I (Chris) say, "Lord, let me love You more than I did yesterday. Let me have more hope than I did yesterday. Let me have more faith than I did yesterday. Let me be everything You need me to be toward those around me today." The last part of that prayer is my application of St. Paul's wish to "become all things to all men" (1 Cor 9:22). There can certainly be variations to this prayer, but from the very beginning of the day we must pray about how we can further the kingdom of God. We need to be praying about having our eyes, ears, and heart open to the opportunities to bring Christ to the lost and hurting.

When I (Chris) was standing in line at a local grocery store's service counter, the attendant seemed to be overwhelmed. A person was wiring some money, which seemed to be the first time the employee had performed such a task. I was third in a line of people becoming more and more frustrated. The great moment of being next finally came to me, but out of the blue someone appeared in a magical "second line" for some lottery tickets. Needless to say, I was not jumping for joy at the moment, but yet I had a feeling that said, "Just let it go." Finally, it was my turn and I tried my best to greet the employee with a big smile. When I was done I turned to go to find a young man from my youth group about three people behind me. As I walked to my car I thanked God for not allowing me to lose my temper, which I had been close to doing. It could have been an embarrassing scandal for me to have berated the employee in front of that young man.

I (Chris) have added this prayer from Father Jacques Philippe to my morning thoughts: "Inspire me in all my decisions, and never let me neglect any of your inspirations."[41] Praying for the Lord's direction in our morning routine will make us attentive toward moments that He will present to us through the day. Then at night we can examine our day. Yes, we should examine our conscience for our faults and failings but also for those moments that we could have shared the Gospel and did not. If we make this a habit, then the next day we ought to be more attuned to such opportunities. If we can look for ways to effectively evangelize on a *daily* basis, then hearts can be changed every *day*.

When one is truly missionful they will look for opportunities to enter into ***Dialogue*** with people about the faith. On our weekly radio show, *Casting Nets with Tony*

& Chris, we have a brief segment that is the "Challenge of the Week." We ask each listener to do something that might open up the doors to true evangelization. They are simple tasks that may take us out of our comfort zone a little, but nothing like asking someone to stand on a street corner to preach.

These are examples of the challenge questions, observations, or invitations that you should work carefully into your conversations:

- "I'm going to (Mass, adoration, prayer). Are there any intentions I can pray for you?"
- "I prayed for you last night."
- "Could you please pray for me and my family?"
- "God loves you."
- "What are you doing for Lent?"
- "What are you doing to get ready for Christmas?"
- "How is your Advent going?"
- "How have you been blessed by God in your life?"
- "I just wanted to say thank you for being such a good co-worker. God has truly blessed me through you."
- Give someone a Catholic book, CD, or DVD, and then ask them about it a week later.
- Give someone a sacramental (with a brief description) as a gift.

- Tell someone who is wearing a cross or a Christian T-shirt, "Thank you for witnessing to the Faith."

All of these can be easily said or done by any individual no matter how shy he or she may be. Personally, we have used these many times. Sometimes conversations begin and other times they do not. Imagine these as just a little knock at the door. Allow the other person to welcome you in, or try again later.

Another opportunity for dialogue occurs in what we call "Human Moments" and "Catholic Moments." "Human Moments" are times when circumstances cause people to become more open to talking about faith. These could be good times such as a child being born, or sad times such as a job loss. In these times a person might be more open toto a conversation about prayer. Here are examples of "Human Moments":

- Birth of a child/grandchild
- A death of a family member or friend
- A marriage or a divorce
- Loss of a job or the gain of new employment
- Retirement
- Graduating from school
- Diagnosis of a disease or sickness
- Moving

These can be described as transitional times in a person's life in which they may be more open to looking at their life from a different perspective. Perhaps they may be willing to look at it with the eyes of eternity. As they open the door of opportunity, go ahead and give it a little knock.

"Catholic Moments" happen when the Faith receives more than normal attention in the secular world. Again, good moments for the Church may occur such as a papal visit, or bad moments such as a priest sexual scandal. As the mainstream media report such events, we can start a conversation by simply asking, "Did you hear about ________?" or "What do you think of _______?" Here are examples of "Catholic Moments":

- Papal deaths/conclaves/visits/news
- Easter/Christmas/Ash Wednesday/Lent/ Halloween
- Release of religious movies (even if they are not favorable to the Church)
- Church scandals
- First Communions
- Weddings
- Funerals
- Baptisms

Talking about spiritual topics becomes easier at such moments, even with people who never talk "religion." Go ahead and experiment with such conversations and pray that the Holy Spirit will lead a dialogue that can bring a new hope and life.

The call to be missionful is the call to go ***Deeper*** in every part of our faith. The New Evangelization is about us growing in our faith in order to communicate with others in a more profound and powerful way. It is about calling those around us to go deeper as well, no matter where they are currently in their spiritual lives. For this reason evangelization will never be a "program" because each person is a unique individual. And thus we must treat them as such. Jesus spoke to people differently: some He yelled at (see Mt 23:13-36), some He engaged in long conversations at night (see Jn 3:1-21), and some He spoke to so compassionately that it upset others (see Lk 7:36-50). We need to live in the same Holy Spirit so that we can treat and speak to those around us the way Our Lord would himself.

Tony and I led a group of young men that we named the Knights of the Holy Queen. We invited guys who were struggling on the weekends with chastity, sobriety, or their faith in general, but who we knew were good men who came from good families. We were not necessarily looking for high school men who were praying the Divine Office every day. Once those men started coming to Mass once a week with us, we then invited them to go deeper by going to confession or going on a retreat. As they went on the retreat and showed commitment by attending Mass regularly, we then invited them to consecrate their life to Jesus Christ through Mary. After they were consecrated and "knighted," we challenged them to go deeper by praying a daily Rosary, worshiping at daily Mass, or saying the Liturgy of the Hours. And we urged them to pray about who they were going to invite to the Knights—and then do it.

Everyone is always "somewhere" in their spiritual journey whether they know it or not. Our calling to be missionful is to help them go deeper, to help them get from "somewhere" to "someone" who is Jesus Christ.

By being committed to being missionful every day we will be instruments available for the Lord to use when and how He wants. We will be able to enter into authentic dialogues that can introduce truth, beauty, and goodness into a world that struggles through darkness and despair. By living in the Holy Spirit we will be able to recognize where people are at and call them to a deeper life with the Triune God. And if we can do that, then we can help them become disciples who will be full of mission bringing the joy of the Gospel to more people every day.

Conclusion

When we give talks about the obligation to evangelize, *The Seven Pillars*, the what-to-dos, and the what-not-to-dos, we always make ourselves available for as long as possible after the presentation to talk with people. It is exciting to hear the stories of their coming to the Faith that has changed both their lives and also their experiences of sharing the Faith. However, no matter how excited we might get someone about evangelization, they commonly resist action with the "but statement":

- "I really enjoyed your talk and would love to evangelize, but ..."
- "I want to talk about the Faith at my work, but ..."
- "My son has left the Faith and I want to invite him to come back to Church, but ..."

We hear one excuse after another. Therefore, in this closing reflection we want to remove all obstacles hindering us from being the instruments of the New Evangelization. Perhaps you still have some hesitations in sharing your faith, and some of these excuses will resonant with you. Or perhaps when you share *The Seven Pillars* with others you might just hear some of the following excuses yourself.

I don't know enough./I don't have a theology degree.

First of all, that is an honest assessment of everyone's faith. We have already stressed that when it comes to knowing the infinite almighty God there will never be a time in which we cannot learn something new. So this excuse should serve as a great challenge to study our faith even more.

Second, we are often sharing the Gospel with individuals who are not Catholic or no longer practicing the Catholic faith. So, this might be a shocking fact, but you will almost always know more about Catholicism than the person you are speaking with. You know what to do with holy water, when to sit and stand during Mass, or how to say the Prayer Before Meals. You may not know more about economic policies or astrophysics, but when it comes to Catholicism you will know more than they do.

Finally, we would never ask you to share "what you don't know," but we are asking you to share "what you *do* know." You should avoid discussing issues that you are not certain about. For example, if you are uninformed about priestly celibacy, you should not answer the question, "Why can't priests get married?" Rather, respond like this: "I know that is a long-standing practice, but I just do not know how it came about or why we still do that. Let me find the answer and get back with you." In that simple answer you have shown integrity.

I'm not holy enough.

Well … that is true for each and every one of us. Thus that statement challenges us to pursue holiness relentlessly every day. However, not being holy enough today does not excuse us from evangelizing. God has, can, and will use imperfect instruments to accomplish His will. If the apostles had waited in the Upper Room until they were holy enough to preach the Gospel, they would still be in there.

I (Tony) remember holding my firstborn child and being overwhelmed with the awareness of my own unworthiness. Here is a precious, beautiful baby girl, and here I am with all my faults and sinfulness. Who am I to take care of her? How can I lead her to her heavenly Father when I struggle with my own temptations? The work of bringing souls to Christ carries the same kind of weight and feelings of unworthiness. However, remember that the work of evangelization is God's work and not ours. We must trust that the Lord will give us the words, virtues, talents, and inspirations that we need in order to spread the kingdom of God.

I can't speak/debate. I get embarrassed. I'm shy.

Remember that elegant words are not as important as sharing the truth with clarity, conviction, and charity. A priest friend of mine (Tony) shared how he invited some missionaries from the Latter-day Saints into his house. He said they had a great conversation in which he was able to use his Greek Bible and even his Hebrew Bible to demonstrate the faithfulness of the Catholic Church to the teachings of Jesus Christ. At the end of the discussion one of the missionaries declared: "I have listened to what you have shared. You are a learned man and what you say I cannot find fault in, but I know that I am right and you are wrong." He left the priest's rectory not Catholic. The elegant words did not work.

The same priest shared another story with me. He had a habit of enjoying coffee on the front porch, and every day a tough-looking young man walked by the rectory. Every day Father would give him some kind welcome, "Good morning," "Have a great day," or "Great to see you." Then the young man stopped walking by the rectory because he had been incarcerated for selling drugs. While he was in jail, he started going to prison ministry, and a Baptist pastor reached out to this young man and was the instrument to introduce Christ into his life.

When the young man was released, the Baptist pastor asked if he would like to join his congregation. He responded "No," but that he wanted to join the Catholic Church. Somewhat bewildered, the pastor asked why he wanted to be Catholic, and he responded, "Because you took interest in me after I started coming to prison ministry, but that Catholic priest was the only one who showed kindness to me even when I didn't deserve it." The young man is still an active member of my friend's parish and has a beautiful family.

The point of the two stories is that it was the same priest who was doing what he was inspired to do to evangelize, but the results are the work of the Holy Spirit.

Finally, we want to point out that we are normally not embarrassed or shy when we talk about those people or things that are important to us. Go to any mall to see countless people wearing their favorite college or sports team apparel, then talk to them about how their team is doing. You may not get away for a while. We expect people to share with us those topics that are close to their hearts. In evangelization, all we are asking you to do is to share the One who is closest to your heart. Clarity, conviction, and charity will always win out.

I'm not a salesman.

Many of us do not have the skills of a great salesman. However, what if you knew that the "product" you were selling was the best of its kind, that nothing else could even compare? What if you knew that every single person in the world needed your "product" and it would make everyone's life better? What if you knew that every person actually wanted your "product" even if they did not yet know the name of your "product"? Let us let you in on a little secret: There is nothing comparable to the greatness of Jesus Christ. He will make everyone's life better, and His image is what every person was created to be. This should send us out with great confidence.

Second, demonstrating a product's effectiveness is the greatest sales tactic. Companies spend millions on billboards, radio ads, and television ads. These ads must be effective because businesses use them, but in my (Chris') personal experience I have never gotten up to go grab some chips after seeing a Doritos commercial. But I will admit that I am a fool for the TV infomercials. If it were not for my wife, the house would be full of these products. Why are infomercials so successful? Because they demonstrate their product. They show us a knife that can cut through a steel pipe and then cut a tomato into paper-thin slices. However, maybe that is just a camera trick. Every year my (Chris') family goes to the state fair and there is a salesman demonstrating the knives to the public. Right in front of our eyes he cuts the steel pipe and then the tomato. Once the demonstration is over the salesman cannot take the money fast enough.

When the product is demonstrated in front of someone it will always be more impressive. We must carry our Christian joy, hope, gratitude, and love to the world. We are the walking billboards, the TV commercials, the infomercials for Christianity. More importantly, we are like the state-fair salesman demonstrating to the world what it means to be a Christian and how it is a life worth buying into.

I don't have time.

One of the most common answers to the greeting "How are you?" has become "Busy." We are always pressed for time. However, there is a difference between "taking the time" and "making the time." We will "make the time" for the things that we are really passionate about. And we must make time for evangelization because eternity is on the line. No one knows when we will have the last chance to share the Gospel with someone. We need to keep in mind that today is the most important day for sharing the Good News. Do not wait.

Second, remember that we must make evangelization a part of our daily life and routine. We do not want evangelization simply to become a program in which we occasionally schedule events. That works well for a parish, but for an individual sharing the Gospel must be like the air that we breathe. We can incorporate evangelization into our trips to the grocery store, dinners, sporting events, or family outings. The time to do it is whenever and wherever we are and the Holy Spirit moves us.

I already do my part. I give money. I already did my work for the Church.

When it comes to our life with God and extending the Kingdom, our work is never finished. While I (Chris) have not made it to fifty years of marriage just yet, I am assuming that once I get there I do not get a card that says, "You don't have to try anymore." There is always something else we can do. The Lord has given us a very specific task, and if we do not do it, it will not get done. There are people in this world who you and only you can reach.

Second, giving money to the work of evangelization is not a replacement for the personal work of evangelization. We can do our work at Casting Nets Ministries because of the generous donations of individuals dedicated to the work of the New Evangelization. However, we remind our benefactors that they still have their own evangelization to do. We have a feeling that on judgment day the Lord is going to ask: "Whom did you clothe? Whom did you feed? Whom did you visit?" He is not going to ask, "How much did you give to clothe, feed, or visit?" We each must reach those who the Lord brings to us.

I'm afraid.

We think that all the above excuses have this one somewhere within it; this is really what it comes down to. Every person is afraid of rejection. We are afraid of being labeled intolerant or pushy. We might fear confrontation. We are afraid that if we push too hard our family and friends will not speak to us. We fear what they may say to us, or even what they may think of us. These are fears that are natural and, we bet, that even the saints struggled with.

I (Tony) am very afraid of fire. Fire is a destructive force that destroys what it touches and causes pain as it consumes. If my house were on fire I would run out in fear. However, if I found out that one of my children was still in the house then the game is changed. I am a large man; 6 feet 4 inches and about two hundred fifty pounds. It would take many large firemen to try to prevent me from running back into the house. The fear of fire would seem as nothing compared to the love I have for my children. Do we love our neighbor, stranger, co-worker, friend, or family enough to walk into a burning building? Do we love them enough to share a Gospel that can save them and bring them to eternal happiness? Love changes everything.

"After this Jesus, knowing that all was now finished, said (to fulfill the Scripture), 'I thirst'" (Jn 19:28). Much has been written about what Jesus meant by this short request He gave from His throne, which was the cross. We believe that Jesus was thirsting for you and me. By giving ourselves completely to Jesus Christ we can help quench His thirst. But we have been given such a precious challenge. Can we bring others to the life-giving waters? Can we help bring people to the Waters of Eternal Life? Thereby we can quench their thirst, and we can help respond to the Savior of the World's request, "I thirst."

Epilogue

After presenting *The Seven Pillars of Effective Evangelization* to a Legatus Chapter we gave the audience the opportunity to ask us questions. The first question asked was, "If you had to add one more pillar to the seven, what would the eighth pillar be?"

We considered that for a moment. Maybe an attitude, such as joy. Or sacrifice. Or gratitude, which each of us should possess in order to attract others to the Faith. But we do not consider these "pillars." As important as these kinds of virtues can be, they are habits that should spread across the "pillars."

Then I (Chris) said, "The Star of the New Evangelization is the Blessed Virgin Mary. If I had to add one more—but I'm not going to—then the eighth pillar would be Mary, the Mother of God." As much as we might desire for our loved ones to come back to the Church or come to Jesus Christ, our desire does not even begin to compare to hers.

There is a "woman" that bookends the Holy Scriptures. In Genesis 3:15 there is a woman whom God will set at enmity with the serpent. At the end of the Bible, in Revelation 12:1–6, there appears a woman who gives birth to the ruler of all the nations.

A "woman" also bookends the Gospel of John. In John 2:1-2, Jesus' mother is attentive to the needs of her neighbors, which brings forth the first miracle of her Son. Then at the end of the Gospel, in John 19:25–27, Jesus, from His cross, gives over the care of His mother to the Beloved Disciple and in turns gives His mother to all of us.

The Blessed Virgin Mary is the woman in all of these texts. According to Scripture and the Church, she plays a unique role in salvation history and continues to play a role in salvation today.

St. John Paul II, the first pontiff to call us to the New Evangelization, gave himself, his work, and his entire pontificate to Mary. The famous motto that was on his coat of arms, "*Totus Tuus*," is an abbreviated form of the St. Louis de Montfort prayer: "I am all yours, and all that I have is yours. May you be my guide in everything."[42] St. John Paul believed that the mother of Christ would be an effective instrument for the New Evangelization. In an exhortation to the Church in the Americas, he said, "It is my heartfelt hope that she, whose intercession was responsible for strengthening the faith of the first disciples (cf. Jn 2:11), will by her maternal intercession guide the Church in America, obtaining the outpouring of the Holy Spirit, as she once did for the early Church (cf. Acts 1:14), so that the new evangelization may yield a splendid flowering of Christian life."[43]

For St. John Paul, the work of the New Evangelization and the devotion to the Blessed Virgin Mary went hand in hand: "I have often invoked her as the 'Star of the New Evangelization'. Now I point to Mary once again as the radiant dawn and sure guide for our steps."[44]

We, too, must invite Mary into every part of our work of bringing the Gospel to others.

Pope Francis notes: "There is a Marian 'style' to the Church's work of evangelization. Whenever we look to Mary, we come to believe once again in the revolutionary nature of love and tenderness."[45] Her life radiates humility and strength. She was quiet and yet spoke with authority. She was obedient and always quick to act. And when Mary acted she always brought others closer to Jesus Christ her son. There is no better example of the perfect disciple for us to model than Mary, the mother of Jesus.

We realize that a total consecration to Jesus Christ through the Blessed Virgin Mary in the style of St. Louis de Montfort is an act of personal devotion. It is not and cannot be considered obligatory for a Catholic to be holy or saintly, or to enter heaven. But we highly encourage such an act of devotion for those involved in the New Evangelization. Following the footsteps of St. Bernard, St. Louis de Montfort, St. Maximilian Kolbe, St. John Paul II, and others, we have personally made the Consecration to Mary. We constantly place all of our efforts into her hands so that she may protect them and make them fruitful. We offer to her care all those we are trying to reach with the Gospel. Remember, she loves those souls and desires their good more than we ever could imagine.

Let us join in prayer with Pope Francis to give over all our work to the Star of the New Evangelization, so she can make our evangelization effective, and bring the maximum number of souls to the Lord Jesus Christ:

Mary, Virgin and Mother,
you who, moved by the Holy Spirit,
welcomed the word of life
in the depths of your humble faith:
as you gave yourself completely to the Eternal One,
help us to say our own "yes"
to the urgent call, as pressing as ever,
to proclaim the good news of Jesus.

Filled with Christ's presence,
you brought joy to John the Baptist,

making him exult in the womb of his mother.
Brimming over with joy,
you sang of the great things done by God.
Standing at the foot of the cross
with unyielding faith,
you received the joyful comfort of the resurrection,
and joined the disciples in awaiting the Spirit
so that the evangelizing Church might be born.

Obtain for us now a new ardor born of the resurrection,
that we may bring to all the Gospel of life
which triumphs over death.
Give us a holy courage to seek new paths,
that the gift of unfading beauty
may reach every man and woman.

Virgin of listening and contemplation,
Mother of love, Bride of the eternal wedding feast,
pray for the Church, whose pure icon you are,
that she may never be closed in on herself
or lose her passion for establishing God's kingdom.

Star of the new evangelization,
help us to bear radiant witness to communion,
service, ardent and generous faith,
justice and love of the poor,
that the joy of the Gospel
may reach to the ends of the earth,
illuminating even the fringes of our world.

Mother of the living Gospel,
wellspring of happiness for God's little ones,
pray for us.

Amen. Alleluia![46]

Appendix A—The Kerygma

How would you answer this question: "You have a minute to give me the core of Christianity, what is it that you believe? What is the Good News?"

We believe the majority of Catholics would struggle with this question. Even for Catholics who are dynamically active in their faith or those with theology degrees, this is a daunting question. For most of us we see the entirety of the Faith almost as a panorama. When we think of the Roman Catholic Church we see the pope (and perhaps past popes), beautiful churches, the Vatican, our pastor, religious sisters, hospitals, soup kitchens, rosaries, statues, the confessional, our first Communion, the Mass, and the list can go on and on. However, to summarize all of that into one minute is impossible for us and would not be helpful for the unbeliever.

We call the core of what we believe the kerygma, which comes from the Greek word meaning "proclamation" or "announcement." Many times we associate the word *gospel*, which means Good News, with kerygma. So what is the "Good News" that we are "proclaiming" to the world? Perhaps you have heard one of our Protestant brethren give this simple description: you are a sinner; Christ died for your sins and rose from the dead; accept Him as your Savior and be saved. There is nothing in this nutshell of the kerygma that we as Catholics would disagree with, but we would like to add a few details as well.

When Archbishop Michael Jackels was the ordinary for the Diocese of Wichita, Kansas, he gave a homily describing the kerygma that made it easy to understand and remember. The first time we heard it, we said to ourselves, "That needs to be in print." With the permission of Bishop Jackels we put his homily into two booklets: *Discover the Truth at Hand*, which is written for non-Christians, and *Remember the Truth at Hand*, which is written for Catholics who are not practicing their faith. They were meant to be purchased in bulk so that the faithful would be willing to pass them out as freely as possible.[47] However, there was another purpose to the booklets, which is for Catholics to have a succinct way to remember and present the Gospel. And all you need to recall the kerygma is already right in your hands. Looking at your left hand:

The Pinky:

> Like the pinky we are weak and small. While God created everything out of love and He loves us, we have sinned and turned away from God.

The Ring Finger:

> Just like we wear a wedding ring, so the Second Person of the Trinity was "wedded" to humanity. The Father sent His only begotten Son to become one with us in the Incarnation, to draw near to us. Jesus was fully God and fully man.

The Middle Finger:

> Like the highest finger, so, too, was Jesus Christ raised high on the cross to pay for our sins. Through His suffering and death our sins can be forgiven, and through His resurrection we can have hope in eternal life.

The Index Finger:

> Like the index finger can be used to point and invite someone to come over, so does Jesus Christ invite us to accept His mercy, life, and love. We must say "Yes" to His plan of salvation.

The Thumb:

> Like the thumb is used by a baseball umpire to single that someone is out, so does this plan of salvation imply that we must get "out" of our old life. We must repent from our sins and follow Christ.

That is the kerygma, the Gospel, the Good News in a nutshell.

However, we know that there is more to the story. So looking at your right hand:

The Pinky:

> Like the pinky we are weak and small so we need to pray every day. Our relationship with the Lord will be made strong through regular communication in a prayer life.

The Ring Finger:

> Like the wedding ring that is the outward sign of a real union, so does Jesus give us a sign of real union. The Lord desires to be so close to us that He gives himself to us at every Mass in the Eucharist, what is also called holy Communion.

The Middle Finger:

> Like the highest finger represents Christ raised on the cross, so does it represent the need for us to take our sins to Him. We have a need to confess our sins, so Jesus gave us the Sacrament of Reconciliation where we can be healed of our transgressions.

The Index Finger:

> Like the index finger invites us to accept Christ, it also represents an invitation for us to know Him. We can come to know Jesus through the Scriptures, but also through the teachings of His Church, which can be found in the *Catechism of the Catholic Church.*

The Thumb:

> Like the thumb is used by a hitchhiker to ask, "Are you going my way," so, too, must a true disciple of Jesus Christ ask others to come along with them in this great adventure towards eternal life.

If we then put our two hands together we will be in a familiar position of prayer. Let us pray that we can be effective instruments to clearly declare the kerygma and bring others to the Good News of Jesus Christ.

Appendix B—Your Testimony

You are sitting on a plane when the person next to you notices the cross you are wearing and asks, "So why are you Christian?" In that moment will you be able to respond in such a way that makes sense to another human being? More importantly, will your response be a moment of grace that invites the questioner into a relationship with Jesus Christ and His Church? Or will you act as if you did not hear the question and hope the person does not repeat it?

As St. Peter said, "Always be prepared to make a defense to anyone who calls you to account for the hope that is in you, yet do it with gentleness and reverence" (1 Pt 3:15). In other words, we must be prepared to give a reason why we believe what we believe. What accounts for the hope that we have? Only Jesus Christ. But how well can we articulate that point to another person? Can we give our story of our life in Christ to someone we know or even someone we do not know? Can we give our "testimony"?

In secular usage, "testimony" is commonly used when a person is called into a court of law as a witness. The witness is asked to give his personal story of the events that he experienced. The witness is placed under oath, swearing that his testimony is true. Our Christian testimony works the same. We act as a witness to testify to the truth of the risen Lord and what He has done in our life.

So can we do that? If we cannot we must work on it. Sharing a testimony effectively takes much thought, much prayer, and much practice. Below we have given a list of six steps that a testimony should contain. Each step requires serious reflection and prayer. If you do these steps we can promise it will be a great spiritual exercise and benefit for you personally and hopefully for those with whom you share.

Begin with a description of your life without Christ: What was it like before coming to realize God's power and presence in your life?

> This is what life was like before "conversion." Now, our "conversion" does not have to be an Augustinian playboy-to-priest story. It does not even have to be something "exciting" or "interesting," it just needs to be your story. Whether we were a cradle Catholic or an atheist, there was a time in which we were not aware of Christ in our lives. However, we warn you not to glamorize sin. You do not need to give details, you are not confessing to a priest. We can make known our struggles without scandal or giving the impression that a life without Christ was "fun" or something that we miss.

Focus on Christ's devotion and fidelity to you: What has God done for you even when you perhaps did not recognize His hand?

> These can be big things or small things. It could be the time that Christ saved your life from an oncoming train, or the time that Christ helped you wake up in the morning when the alarm did not go off. The point is to reflect upon the times in which God was active in your life even in the midst of sin or during times when you did not even notice it. The hope is

that perhaps the person listening will recognize how God might be working in his or her life right now.

Describe how the Holy Spirit was always there prodding: How did God show that He was never giving up on you?

Even when we did not have Christ in our lives personally, we experienced this constant nudging. Again this could be small things or big things, perhaps a retreat or a kind act from someone. The point is that even when we thought we were getting away from God He was gently pulling us closer to himself. Christ never stops pursuing us.

Share the "key to change" in your life, that is Jesus Christ: What was the moment of the change or when you did come to know Jesus?

All of the above details changed when Jesus became the center of our lives. Even people who have always had some knowledge of Jesus usually come to the point of giving their lives fully to Him. He is the reason for the change, the happiness and peace that we now have. Neither our will nor some 12-step program could bring about such a change, but only the Living God and His grace.

Describe the change God has made in your life: What difference does Jesus make in your life?

Finally, we get to the really good stuff, which is how our lives are now different. God brought us out of all our sins. Life without grave sin is possible if we rely on His grace. Now you describe your daily prayer life, how much more you get out of Mass, and how the Bible has come to life. Describe how the desire to serve others has filled your heart, how you have many faith-filled relationships, and are certain that God is on your side fighting temptations. Our lives can be filled with peace, joy, and happiness. That is change we can all believe in.

Explain that you still have problems, difficulties, but God has given you the power to follow Him: What is it like to be a Christian today?

Even though we have given everything to Christ we are still in the process of change. Conversion is not a one-time event but is an everyday continual process. Every day we must make a decision to live for Christ and in His Church. Every day we need to turn away from sin, but we are confident that Christ will continue to work in our lives and through the graces He pours upon us through His Church, and we will continue to grow closer to Him.

Spend a good amount of time on each of the six steps. Write your testimony down. It is highly encouraged that you develop different lengths of your story. Have one that is about three minutes long, one that is fifteen minutes long, and maybe even one that is about an hour. The reason for this is that in real life we will not have a set time; each experience will be different and we must be ready. Finally, once you have done all of this, share it with someone. It can be someone you know who knows your story or a stranger, but practice it so that you can truly learn to articulate the marvels that Christ has accomplished in your life.

Casting Nets Ministries, Inc.
1117 Hazelwood
Wichita, KS 67212
(316) 619-0497
www.CastingNetsOnline.com
chris@castingnetsonline.com

Notes

1 *Evangelii Nuntiandi*, 5.

2 World Mission Day, 1991.

3 *Decree on the Apostolate of the Laity*, 2.

4 World Mission Day, 2007.

5 *Catechism of the Catholic Church*, 1816.

6 *Spe Salvi*, 48.

7 *Disciples Called to Witness*, 9.

8 Hahn, Scott, talk "Rebuilding the Christian Civilization" (Lighthouse Catholic Media, 2006).

9 Pope Francis, *Evangelii Gaudium*, 259 (emphasis added).

10 Dom Jean-Baptiste Chautard, *The Soul of the Apostolate* (Rockford: TAN Publishers, 1946), 39.

11 Ibid., 39.

12 "Is there anyone who does not know St. Bernard's saying, to apostles, 'If you are wise, you will be reservoirs and not channels.' The channels let the water flow away, and do not retain a drop. But the reservoir is first filled, and then, without emptying itself, pours out its overflow, which is ever renewed, over the fields which it waters. How many there are devoted to works, who are never anything but channels, and retain nothing for themselves, but remain dry while trying to pass on life-giving grace to souls! 'We have many channels in the Church today,' St. Bernard added, sadly, 'but very few reservoirs.'" *The Soul of the Apostolate*, 53.

13 *Evangelii Gaudium*, 281.

14 Ibid., 3.

15 Ibid., 101.

16 Ibid., 128.

17 *Spe Salvi*, 48.

18 These prayers are available as beautiful bookmarks at www.CastingNetsOnline.com.

19 St. Benedict, *The Rule of St. Benedict*, (New York: Image Books, 1975), 89, 90.

20 St. Augustine, *The Confessions* (New York: Image Books, 1960), 43.

21 April 25, 2005 (translated from the Spanish version).

22 For more information about Servant of God Father Emil Kapaun: www.frkapaun.org; "The Story of Chaplain Kapaun," by Msgr. Arthur Tonne; "A Shepherd in Combat Boots," by William Maher; "A Saint Among Us," by The Father Kapaun Guild.

23 *Saturday Evening Post*, January 16, 1954.

24 *Spe Salvi*, 2.

25 *Evangelii Gaudium*, 121.
26 Ibid., 8.
27 Ibid., 24.
28 *Sacrosanctum Concilium*, 2.
29 *The Soul of the Apostolate*, 186.
30 Ibid., 185.
31 Ralph Martin and Peter Williamson, *John Paul II and the New Evangelization* (Cincinnati: Servant Books, 2006), 209.
32 *Evangelii Gaudium*, 264.
33 Address to the Synod of Bishops, November 12, 2012.
34 *Evangelii Gaudium*, 44.
35 General Audience, February 19, 2014.
36 Proposition 28.
37 *Catechesi Tradendae,* 19 (emphasis added).
38 We invented the word "Missionful" so that it fit with the other Pillars.
39 *Evangelii Nuntiandi*, 14.
40 *Lineamenta*, 10.
41 *In the School of the Holy Spirit* (Scepter: New York, 2007), 29.
42 Homily, December 8, 1978.
43 *Ecclesia in America*, 11.
44 *Novo Millennio Ineunte*, 58.
45 *Evangelii Gaudium*, 288: "There is a Marian 'style' to the Church's work of evangelization. Whenever we look to Mary, we come to believe once again in the revolutionary nature of love and tenderness. In her we see that humility and tenderness are not virtues of the weak but of the strong who need not treat others poorly in order to feel important themselves. Contemplating Mary, we realize that she who praised God for 'bringing down the mighty from their thrones' and 'sending the rich away empty' (Lk 1:52-53) is also the one who brings a homely warmth to our pursuit of justice. She is also the one who carefully keeps 'all these things, pondering them in her heart" (Lk 2:19). Mary is able to recognize the traces of God's Spirit in events great and small. She constantly contemplates the mystery of God in our world, in human history and in our daily lives. She is the woman of prayer and work in Nazareth, and she is also Our Lady of Help, who sets out from her town 'with haste' (Lk 1:39) to be of service to others. This interplay of justice and tenderness, of contemplation and concern for others, is what makes the ecclesial community look to Mary as a model of evangelization. We implore her maternal intercession that the Church may become a home for many peoples, a mother for all peoples, and that the way may be opened to the birth of a new world. It is the Risen Christ who tells us, with a power that fills us with confidence and unshakeable hope: 'Behold, I make all things new' (Rev 21:5)."
46 *Evangelii Gaudium*, 288.
47 The Truth at Hand Project can be found at_www.CastingNetsOnline.com/about-truth-at-hand.